"*Praying for Boys* is more than a book of prayers or a devotional book for moms. It's a real toolbox that empowers parents to lead, love, and fight for the hearts of their sons. It's brought me to my knees, not in desperation but in excitement!"

—Amanda White, ohAmanda.com,
author of *Truth in the Tinsel*

"*Praying for Boys* is profoundly motivating and biblical. Every mom who needs direction in raising boys into spiritually vibrant men will be challenged to embrace this clear strategy that Brooke provides. Highly practical and very encouraging!"

—Sally Clarkson, director of Mom Heart Ministries
and author of *Desperate*

"What a gift Brooke has given us in this wonderfully practical and urgently needed book. We all want the very best for our sons. We invest so much in growing our boys up right, but we must remember that only our prayer partnership with God can mold their hearts. Brooke teaches us mamas how to fill the most sacred spaces of parenting with powerfully effective prayers."

—Lysa TerKeurst, *New York Times* bestselling author
and president of Proverbs 31 Ministries

"I can't think of a greater resource for parents of boys than this book. Brooke McGlothlin has taken her love for all things boy, spelled out the important stuff, and infused a deep understanding of what boys need most in these pages. It is a must-read and pass-it-on kind of book!"

—Lisa Whittle, speaker and author of {w}hole

"Brooke's words on prayer have been an inspiration to me as I raise three boys. *Praying for Boys* has challenged me to get on my knees and cry out to God for my sons in ways I never had before—boldly, expectantly, persistently, passionately. My mama heart has been changed."

—Erin Mohring, co-founder of Raising Boys Media

"As a mom it is a necessity and a privilege to bring our children to God through prayer. Brooke has created a fantastic resource to encourage and help us along the way. *Praying for Boys* is a must-have for every boy-mom!"

—Ruth Schwenk, speaker, writer,
and creator of thebettermom.com

"With a heart for praying God's Word and a vision for raising up the next generation of godly men, I've been given a gift through Brooke's *Praying for Boys*. With three teen sons, I yearn for authentic encouragement and biblical wisdom that points me to the cross—Brooke does just that."

—Jen Schmidt, author of the blog,
Balancing Beauty and Bedlam

"While our sons grow tall, wearing out the knees on their jeans from tumble and play, we mothers too find our fabric worn thin from kneeling in prayer for our soon-to-be men. Brooke's practical book, full of vulnerable sharing and deeply rooted in God's Word, will become a useful tool as you seek to make prayer a priority and model for your boys just how to run hard after Jesus."

—Karen Ehman, Proverbs 31 Ministries director of speakers
and author of *LET. IT. GO.*

Brooke McGlothlin is co-founder of the popular online community for mothers of boys, the MOB Society (www.themobsociety.com). She received her B.S. in Psychology from Virginia Tech in 1999 (Go Hokies!), Masters in Counseling from Liberty University in 2003, and served more than fourteen years in local pregnancy-care ministry before making the best choice of her life—staying home with her boys. She's the author of several books and resources for moms, and currently resides in the mountains of southwest Virginia with her husband—the man she's had a crush on since the third grade—their two sons, and two Labs, Toby and Siri. Learn more about Brooke at www.brookemcglothlin.com.

Praying for Boys

Praying for Boys

ASKING GOD
FOR THE THINGS THEY NEED MOST

Brooke McGlothlin

BETHANY HOUSE PUBLISHERS
a division of Baker Publishing Group
Minneapolis, Minnesota

Portions of this text were previously published in *Warrior Prayers* (2011)

Published by Bethany House Publishers
11400 Hampshire Avenue South
Bloomington, Minnesota 55438
www.bethanyhouse.com

Bethany House Publishers is a division of
Baker Publishing Group, Grand Rapids, Michigan

Printed in the United States of America

Library of Congress Cataloging-in-Publication Data
McGlothlin, Brooke.
    Praying for boys : asking God for the things they need most / Brooke McGlothlin.
        pages cm
    Includes bibliographical references.
    Summary: "With uplifting stories and Bible-based prompts, the leader of a thriving online community teaches moms how to pray for the areas their sons struggle with most"— Provided by publisher.
    ISBN 978-0-7642-1143-0 (pbk. : alk. paper)
    1. Mothers—Religious life. 2. Intercessory prayer—Christianity. 3. Sons—Psychology. 4. Boys—Psychology. I. Title.
BV4529.18.M37 2014
242'.6431—dc23   2013034264

Unless otherwise indicated, Scripture quotations are from The Holy Bible, English Standard Version® (ESV®), copyright © 2001 by Crossway, a publishing ministry of Good News Publishers. Used by permission. All rights reserved. ESV Text Edition: 2007

Scripture quotations identified NLT are from the *Holy Bible*, New Living Translation, copyright © 1996, 2004, 2007 by Tyndale House Foundation. Used by permission of Tyndale House Publishers, Inc., Carol Stream, Illinois 60188. All rights reserved.

Cover design by Dan Pitts

Author is represented by MacGregor Literary, Inc.

16 17 18 19 20 21 22   11 10 9 8 7 6 5

To my grandmothers,

Catherine Trout Lloyd (Cack)
and
Wanda Jewell McDonald (Duel)

Cack, you left three good men behind, including my father, who were the evidence of your sacrifice, deep love, and hard work. Their lives, and the lives of your grandchildren, tell your story. "Thank you" just doesn't cut it.

Duel, thank you for teaching your children and grandchildren the power of prayer. Apparently, it stuck with me. Until heaven . . .

Contents

Contents

Foreword

In *Praying for Boys*, Brooke McGlothlin takes a stand for boys and their well-being, and it's a stand based firmly in the Word of God. It's bold and countercultural, and therefore likely to be controversial. I know Brooke, and I know she doesn't want to create such controversy, but the beauty of this book is in its bravery. These are days that require boldness of purpose and speech, and she does just that.

She affirms boys for who they are and how God created them. Her belief is that the raising of boys as honorable standard-bearers for their faith, family, and community is something to be honored, not condemned. Rare stuff indeed. I commend her for it and admire her courage.

My wife and I prayed over our three sons using this book, and continue to do so. It's made a difference in how we view them and their world. If they grow up knowing that their mother and father are praying Scripture over them, perhaps they will be so conditioned by the training of God's Word that they will allow it to take root in their core, becomingly fiercely dependent on Christ for all things.

Study the verses Brooke references and consider what she writes. I firmly believe it will be a difference-maker as you raise your young men. Nothing is more powerful than the Bible, and rarely has it been so powerfully presented in the raising of boys as within these pages.

Cliff Graham
Author of the *Lion of War* novels and movies

Boys Are a Battle Zone

I watch their little faces as we prepare for bedtime prayers. I'm overwhelmed with love for them—overwhelmed with parenting them, these little boys who have stolen my heart and rocked my world.

As I write this, my sons are seven and five, and I already find myself wondering where the time has gone. I'm running as fast as I can to keep up with every step they take, tucking each moment away in my memory for safekeeping.

I asked God to give me boys. Even before I was married I knew I wanted to raise men who would be different—respecters of women, lovers of God. Men who would work with their hands, take commitments seriously, and protect the least of these. Men who were warriors, protectors, worshipers, peacemakers, and friends.

Fast-forward twelve years or so, and the present-day circus that is my life often finds me asking . . .

WHAT WAS I THINKING?

I don't have any clue how to be a mom of boys! They're rough and tumble; I don't have an athletic bone in my body. They're loud and obnoxious; I enjoy peace and quiet. They love dirt and mud and bugs; I'd rather curl up with a good book in my cool, clean family room.

Obviously, God has a sense of humor.

If you are the mother of at least one boy, you're nodding your head in agreement with me right now. I used to think there was something wrong with my boys, that they were the only ones in the world who acted the way they do. Then the Lord hooked me up with an awesome community of boy-moms, and I learned that this simply isn't true! There *is* something different about boys!

- They're loud.
- They like to leap from tall buildings with no safety net (*aka* jump off the top bunk).
- They like to build forts and hide candy.
- They break toilets and "go" in (and all over) anything BUT the toilet.
- They're adventurous.
- They're natural-born protectors.
- They like to shoot things (even when there's nothing actually resembling a gun).
- They shower you with spit when showcasing their sound-effects skills.
- They love their mommies and need their daddies.
- They're made of snakes and snails and puppy-dog tails. (Okay, not really. But when I told my oldest that girls were made of sugar and spice and everything nice, he asked if he could lick me!)

Raising boys brings one adventure after another, but I'm afraid we're losing the beauty and importance of training up godly men. Churches are filled with men who have no idea what it truly means to be a man. They find their self-worth in their jobs, or their cars, or worse—anywhere except in the Lord.

Our boys need faithful Christian parents now more than ever, and we're failing them. But it doesn't have to be that way. We can choose to rejoin the war for the hearts of our sons . . . today.

But how?

The Battle

In his lifetime, Eli the priest was given three men to train, teach, and raise, but he only got it right with one of them. Samuel came under Eli's care through the prayers of his desperate mother, Hannah. After years of being barren, she "vowed a vow and said, 'O LORD of hosts, if you will indeed look on the affliction of your servant and remember me and not forget your servant, but will give to your servant a son, then I will give him to the LORD all the days of his life'" (1 Samuel 1:11). So Samuel, the fruit of that desperate prayer, spent his childhood with Eli in the temple.

Even as a child Samuel knew and listened to the voice of God. We know him as the man God used to choose the first and second kings of Israel. We can assume Eli trained Samuel in the ways of the Lord. Certainly he helped him to recognize the voice of the Lord (1 Samuel 3). But the Bible says something completely different regarding Eli's biological sons, Hophni and Phinehas. According to 1 Samuel 2:12, Eli's sons were worthless men, unrestrained in their behavior, and Eli did nothing to stop them.

Eli failed to raise his sons to know and fear the Lord, and the cost was heavy.

- While Samuel was ministering to the Lord, Eli's two sons were hindering the people's worship (1 Samuel 2:11–36).
- The Lord cursed Eli's lineage saying, "There will not be an old man in your house" (1 Samuel 2:31).

- Hophni and Phinehas both died on the same day in battle against the Philistines (1 Samuel 4:17).
- The ark of God was captured by the Philistines (1 Samuel 4:17).
- Eli died when he heard the news of his sons' deaths and the capture of the ark (1 Samuel 4:18).
- Eli's daughter-in-law, the wife of Phinehas, went into apparent premature labor and died giving birth (1 Samuel 4:19–22).

Apparently, God takes the way we raise our sons quite seriously.

I don't know about you, but I feel like we're losing our sons. Take a look around. What do you see? Everywhere you look men are leaving the church, leaving their wives, throwing out the Word of God as their main authority. The call of God to raise men to know Him and fear Him still stands. But are we doing that?

I don't think so.

I submit to you that as a culture, we've been more like Eli than we care to admit. Our sons don't know the Father God, because their fathers (and mothers) don't know and trust the Father God. They don't see a big difference between what the world says it means to be a man and what they see in church. Many popular male Christian writers of our time say men in the church don't even know what it means to be godly men. They're bored and tired, and most feel that to align themselves with the teachings of the church means to die to what's in their hearts.

All it takes to lose the truth of the Word of God is one set of parents who fail to teach it. The result can be generations of men who don't know and fear the Lord. Imagine the impact for a moment. It's a lot to take in.

So what do we do about it? How do we make a change? My answer might surprise you.

There are so many books out there today on the topic of parenting that I can't count them. Nor do I have time to read them all. But even if I did, reading these books and putting the solid tools in them to work still doesn't come with guarantees. Refusing to compromise the Word of God as we raise our sons helps tremendously, but it can't change hearts of stone to hearts of flesh.

Knowing this, it becomes quite clear that the best way a mom can enter the war for the heart of her son is on her knees.

Prayer

About four years ago I began praying Scripture over my children. Since then, it has become quite a passion of mine. I love to take the Word and wash it over my boys in prayer, substituting their names in when I can, and asking the Lord to bring it to fruition in their lives.

One day, as I was praying for my boys, the Lord dropped the seed into my heart for this book. So many resources exist out there for girls. There are even some great books that I would wholeheartedly recommend on the subject of prayer for our children. What was missing, I realized, was a book leading mothers in how to pray specifically for their sons in the areas they need it most. Something to equip, encourage, and bless mothers of boys on the journey to raising godly men.

So many of you moms have been kneeling down or lying flat on your face before God, asking Him to help you. You're lost, overwhelmed, exhausted, stressed, heartbroken, and seconds away from waving the white flag in defeat. I know where you are. I've been there. I'm still there. I have no idea how to make this dream of mine come true. I have no idea how to raise men who will be different: respecters of women, lovers of God. I have no idea how to teach little men to work with their hands, take commitments seriously, and protect the least of these. And I certainly have no idea how to raise warriors, protectors, worshipers, peacemakers, and friends by myself.

But I do know how to get down on my knees and cry out to God on their behalf. I do know God's Word is "living and active, sharper than any two-edged sword, piercing to the division of soul and of spirit, of joints and of marrow, and discerning the thoughts and intentions of the heart" (Hebrews 4:12).

I'm convinced prayer is the missing piece of this puzzle. Parents who pray for their children recognize their own inability to change their children's hearts, and put their faith and hope in the God who can. Our best work on our boys' behalf—the *most* important thing we can do for them each and every day—is to wage war on our knees. So I pray the Word over my boys daily, asking the One who has the power to change hearts of stone into hearts of flesh to find my boys and make them His.

If you're looking for a book to teach you how to raise godly men, *Praying for Boys* isn't it. Neither is it a book that promises five easy ways to produce a boy to be proud of. In fact, it isn't really a book about *you* at all. It's a book about the God who loves your son more than you do and wants to work in his heart and life *in spite* of you as you pray and desperately seek Him.

So as we gather our battle gear and get ready to join the fight for our sons, let's take a few minutes to survey the land and get to know what we're up against first. We'll start by gaining a deeper understanding of prayer—why we should do it and how it works.

Ready to fight?

What Is Prayer, and Why Should We Do It?

In the Old Testament book of Judges, a familiar story brims with unfamiliar hope and direction for moms trying to raise godly men. The story of Samson has long been used as a perfect illustration of how the power of God can rest even on those who reject His ways, bringing His perfect will to pass. Any child who grew up attending church remembers the pictures of Samson's huge, muscular frame pushing over the pillars and killing the Philistines. But the lesser known part of that story is that of his parents—another woman visited by an angel of the Lord with news of an impending birth, and a man who begged God for help.

The fact that Samson's mother had been barren had somehow escaped me in spite of years of Sunday school training and Bible study. In the Old Testament days, barrenness was often accompanied by shame and social ridicule, so when Samson's mother was told by the angel that she would bear a son, I imagine she was a little overwhelmed. She and Manoah, her husband, would finally hold a child in their hands! What joy! What grace! What . . . panic?

Birthing babies is a normal part of the day-to-day rhythm of life and has been since the fall of man in the garden of Eden. Women joyfully receive the news of pregnancy and process how it might change their lives every single day. I found out about my pregnancies by using a pregnancy test. Women of Manoah's day might've done it differently, but I daresay most of them were not visited by angels! It's safe to assume this precious couple knew something was going to be different about their baby boy, and in Judges 13:8 we see Manoah crying out to God:

"O Lord, please let the man of God whom you sent come again to us and teach us what we are to do with the child who will be born."

And therein lies the heart of all believing parents who want to raise their children to know and serve the Lord. I can almost feel Manoah's desperation as he pleads with the Lord to help him know what to do with this promised child.

Have you ever felt a bit like Samson's parents? I know I have. In fact, I feel that way most days. Just when I think I have a handle on what to do with my boys, how to raise them or teach them, something happens to mess it all up and I'm left once again begging the same question of God that Manoah and his wife did: "God! Teach me what in the world to do with these sons you've given me!"

My husband and I sat on the beach last summer celebrating ten years of marriage just about the same time I received the news that I would get the honor of writing this book for you. As I listened to the waves hit the beach and dug my toes in the sand, I found myself wondering about the similarities between Samson and my own two boys. Is it right for parents today to cry out to God? To beg Him to show us the way like Samson's parents did?

Our boys may not be just like Samson—designed by God to be fierce and strong, a fighter against those who threatened His chosen people—but they *are* called to fight against the ruler of this world and for God's kingdom here on earth. So what does that mean?

Maybe you and I weren't visited by an angel of the Lord to announce the births of our sons, but the call of God is no less evident on their lives, even if we can't see it yet.

Maybe our sons won't have supernatural physical strength designed to defeat entire armies of men alone, but they *will* be called on to fight the enemy of their souls on a daily basis.

Maybe the story of our sons' lives will only be known to a few instead of many, but the impact their lives can have on those around them is no less profound.

Which leads me to this: We *are* raising men to be warriors for God's kingdom, and I think God expects us to ask Him—no, *beg* Him—to help us know how to do it well. Asking God for help is easier than we make it, and since prayer is the number one way we ask God for help, let's spend a few minutes talking about what prayer really is.

Prayer

Explanations of prayer are often over-spiritualized and over-intellectualized, in my opinion. As a blogger and speaker, I meet people who have been affected by the prayer ministry God's given me. They come to me often and say, "Your prayer book has changed my life" or "God has given you a gift for prayer," as if I have some kind of special anointing from the Lord in this area.

Maybe I do. I don't want to discount the gifts the Lord gives for His specific purposes. But friends, when I was a little girl dreaming about what I would become and how I would use my life for the Lord, being a prayer warrior wasn't even on my radar.

21

My prayer ministry didn't come to me because I worked for it or aspired to it. It didn't come because I had all the right answers or knew an abundance of Scripture by heart. I don't even really like that this book is seen as a parenting book, because I don't consider myself an expert on that subject.

Just like Samson's parents, I pray because I don't know what else to do.

I pray because I don't have all the answers. I pray because I'm lost and can't see the big picture. I pray because I'm desperate for a word-touch from the God who made me and because I can't do this life thing without His direction. I pray because I don't know how to raise these two boys to be the godly men I dream they will be, but I serve the God who does. Believing that has changed my life.

So in the spirit of the confession that prayer is really so much simpler than we make it, let's explore four very small words that sum up what I believe prayer really is: talking, asking, listening, and believing.

Talking to God

I like to call myself a raging introvert. Isn't that a fun pairing of words? A friend recently accused me of being an extrovert because I can talk so passionately (on, and on, and on . . .) about the things I love and stand for. Get me going on the subject of the sanctity of life or saying "yes" to God, and you might mistake me for someone who is energized by people when, in fact, people wear me totally out. Small, quiet spaces with the people I hold most dear energize me best. I guess that's why it's so easy for me to chat with God.

I use the word *chat* intentionally because I believe there's an entire element of prayer that works best in an informal chat-like-a-friend kind of way. Some people call it conversational prayer—the kind where you find yourself telling God about your day as you drive to work, or when you pause during a stress-filled time just to say, "Help me, Lord." Whatever you call it, it's important to remember that God is much closer to us than we might think.

On the day that divided time, God sent Jesus to dwell among men. Now, I know you probably celebrate some part of that each year at Christmas. But I'd like to take a moment to consider the full impact of what the words *dwell among men* could have on our prayer lives.

Have you ever thought about the fact that Jesus lived among men and women just like us? He had a mother and a father, siblings, cousins, and friends. And although all of His conversations with the people He lived with aren't given to us in the Bible, it's safe to assume He laughed, told secrets, listened to His siblings whine about who would get to ride the donkey first, and felt the pressures of living just like we do today. To say there were times when He felt burdened by a friend's loss or by the demands of interacting in a world full of sin is a gross understatement, because we know this is why He came. Jesus stepped down from heaven—a place of peace and perfection—into our messy, sin-filled world because He wanted to be "God with us."

With us.

Not above us. Not up in the clouds somewhere looking down on us. *With* us.

Right now, Jesus is with you—watching you, loving you, listening to you. He knows you more intimately than anyone else and has spent all the days of your life cultivating a relationship with you. Why? Because He loved you enough to die for you.

Friend, no one knows you better than the God who sent His Son to die for you. Close your eyes and imagine Him sitting right beside you, just like an old friend . . . because He is! That's a pretty compelling case for feeling comfortable enough with someone to just chat.

I remember well the first time I talked to Jesus like a friend. I had just broken up with my college boyfriend because I knew the relationship wasn't headed down the right path. He wasn't the one for me, and I knew it, but I cared deeply for him and missed him terribly. I wrestled with God over surrendering my will to His, really for the first time in my life. It was a pivotal time—when I truly began walking closely with the Lord and decided His way was better than mine.

I sat on my bed in my college apartment, crying like a baby and feeling like I had made a mess out of my life. And with my eyes closed and heart open to the Lord like never before, I poured out words to Jesus like He was sitting right next to me on the bed. My tone changed, and instead of praying formal "Thy will be done" prayers, I began to talk to Him like I would my best friend. I experienced a side of this earthly relationship with Jesus I had never experienced before, and when I was done, my life had changed. I felt like I had spent time with someone who knew me and loved me better than anyone else. Indeed, I had.

The New Living Translation of the Bible renders Psalm 116:2 this way: "Because he bends down to listen, I will pray as long as I have breath!" Just knowing the God of the universe has His ear bent toward me and my life is enough to keep my heart open to Him in prayer—oftentimes just simple, conversational prayers that keep me connected to my Father. Let me give you an example of what this might sound like for me on any given day:

"Morning, Savior. Thanks for another day to worship You and be with my loved ones. Thanks for coffee. These boys, Lord . . . they wear me out. I love them to the moon and back, but I need an extra dose of Your strength today. I'm tired, but I want to mother them well. Help me love them even when I don't feel like it. Help me show them who You are. Help me see into their hearts. And Savior, can You help me really *feel* Your presence here with me today, please? I love You, Lord. Talk to You again in about an hour. Amen."

Not rocket science. Just my heart spilled out to the God who bends down to listen to a mama who loves her boys.

Would you try it with me right now, friends? Sit down somewhere (for you moms of little ones . . . go hide in the bathroom and turn the ventilation fan on . . . it helps), close your eyes, breathe in deeply, drown out the noise, and say something like this to your Savior:

"Morning, God. Thanks for another day to worship and serve You. Thanks for really seeing me right now. Help me believe that You love me even when I don't feel like it could be true. Give me and my family grace today as we find our way through this life. Lead us on the path You have for us today. (Insert any specific prayer requests you might have right now.) I love You, Lord. Talk to You again in about an hour. Amen."

Asking God for Help

We touched a bit on asking God for our specific requests as we chat with Him, but I want to more deeply explore the heart of asking for help by giving you an example of some things I have personally been praying for recently.

Homeschooling this past year at the "McGlothlin Home for Boys" was hard. It was our first year homeschooling two boys instead of just one, and it took me months to find a routine that worked for them. Both of my boys rank high on the I-need-Mommy's-attention-to-succeed-O-meter, and both have trouble following through with directions unless I'm sitting right beside them. My oldest, a second-grader then, had made some progress in this area, so I thought I would be able to get him started on his lessons for the day and then work freely with his younger brother, a kindergartner. Not so. Apparently, my oldest had gotten rather fond of snuggling with Mommy while doing his school. And while I love the snuggling too (one of my favorite parts of homeschooling!), this mama's lap is only so big and I am only capable of teaching one subject at a time.

As an introvert, one of my biggest challenges—or hang-ups, if you will—is noise. I can deal with the everyday just-living-life kind of background noise, but the constant boy noise in our house drains me every single day. Multiply the normal amounts of boy noise times two upset kids who both want their mama at the same time and absolutely refuse to wait to ask questions, and you'll get an emotional picture of how I felt for the first four months of the year. On top of all this, my youngest son quickly grew very bored with his kindergarten curriculum. By early November I was fighting him to do even an hour's worth of work. What was supposed to be a fun first year of school for him was quickly becoming a nightmare.

Sometime close to Thanksgiving, after finally getting the boys in bed for the night, I grabbed my Bible, closed our bedroom door, and told my husband I wasn't coming out for a while.

I knelt at my makeshift "altar" (my bed) and told the Lord He needed to remember how little I bring to the table with this parenting gig. I think He smiled a crooked smile as I poured out my heart to Him and begged Him to give me direction and grace. I knew I needed to pray specifically into the situation we were dealing with but wasn't sure how to start.

I opened my hands, surrendering our mess to the only One I trusted to fix it. Something needed to change, and as I reflected on what had become of our homeschooling life, I realized it was probably me. Oh sure, my boys need their hearts changed too, but I can't do that for them. I can only offer God what I have and ask Him to change me and use me as an example for them.

As I prayed for help that night, just simply pouring out my heart to God and then listening to Him in return, I felt a nudge toward pencil and paper. Slowly, I began to make a list of all of the areas I felt needed to change in my heart and the hearts of my sons. Then I gave them a name—a specific, biblical name for the area of sin they represented—and began searching the Scriptures for how to pray into those specific areas. (You can download a short, practical resource to help you do this for yourself and your family at www.prayingfor boys.com/resources.)

The process of surrendering to God, asking Him for help, and then simply opening my ears and heart to His leading was one of the best things I could ever have done. This small but intense prayer session led to some significant changes in how we moved forward with school in the new year. We allowed my youngest son to take a month off of his lessons in order to be able to start fresh with a new curriculum after Christmas, and I was inspired both with a renewed vision for the place and purpose of prayer in our home, and with a new vision for how to engage my sons when things went awry.

You see, God revealed to me that I had been entering the battle *with* my sons, not *for* them. When they had tantrums, I had tantrums (ugly, but true) right back. I was losing my cool, and in my attempts to just get them to stop and obey me, I was actually teaching them to respond exactly the way they were.

Once I understood this, my heart near exploded with the need to repent. And slowly, as I turned away from battling against my sons, I saw things change for the better. It wasn't an easy process. There are still plenty of failures on my part—failures that find me asking my own children to forgive me. But we all have a choice to make any time God reveals our hearts to us— follow His leading, or continue to live in sin. Looking at it like that made the choice somehow a bit easier.

Most of the time, friends, I feel totally unprepared for this battle, and I'm not sure why God has chosen me to fight it in all my average, messy, unorganized glory. But the good news is that asking God for help is as easy as this:

1. Admit all the things we are not.
2. Acknowledge all that God is.
3. Trust His promise that He will make Himself look good through our weaknesses: "My grace is sufficient for you, for my power is made perfect in weakness" (2 Corinthians 12:9).

I've found the best posture of the heart to wear while asking God for help is one of humility. Getting my weaknesses out there between me and God sets me up to accept His truth better, remember my dependence on Him, and give Him the glory for anything good that may come in this life. It reminds me a bit of Joshua. . . .

Joshua and the Israelites marched around the city of Jericho with nothing more than trumpets, and maybe some slingshots, arrows, and spears (Joshua 5). The wall that stood between them and the promise of God must have looked like an enemy far too big for their measly weapons, but their hearts were filled with faith in God, and as it turns out, that's all they really needed.

Their faith inspires me to do my own circling of sorts—through prayer (a concept from Mark Batterson's book *The Circle Maker*[1])—around our homeschool year, around friends and family who are hurting, and around other situations that rest out of my control. Like Joshua, my weapons of warfare fall sadly short of what I think is needed to win the war. But it helps me to remember God hasn't asked me to win. He's only asked me . . . asked you . . . to be faithful in the battle.

1. Mark Batterson, *The Circle Maker* (Grand Rapids, MI: Zondervan, 2011).

So I circle the walls of my own Jericho—that circumstance that's bigger, stronger, and tougher than me—and ask God to make them fall.

And God's crooked smile? I think that's Him reminding me He often chooses the foolish things of the world to shame the wise, and the weak to shame the strong (1 Corinthians 1:27). If so, I'm positioned right where He needs me. You?

"Lord, make something of all this that makes You look good. Use all of my weaknesses to give Yourself glory. Use my mess, and the way You've been so faithful, to meet me in it, to bring another mama hope that You can do the same for her. I love You, Lord. Talk to You in about an hour. Amen."

Just ask, friends—ask and give. Don't worry as much about the answers to your prayers as you do giving them to the One who has the power to work in them. In your asking, remember that God sees you and gave His Son for you, and let that give you the faith to ask again.

Listening to God

In December of 2001, the Lord called me to establish a consistent quiet time. He reasoned with me, and I agreed that if I truly wanted to follow Him, I needed to actually hear from Him. And since His Word tells us that the main way He talks to us nowadays is through His Son (Hebrews 1:2), I figured the best way to hear from Him was to read His Word. Again, not rocket science.

I had spent the previous six months pouring my heart into my very first full-time job. A ministry calling, it didn't take long for me to realize that giving and giving and giving without putting anything back in was forcing me to run on empty. What had started out as a joy for me was becoming a chore, and I was positioning myself to burn out quickly.

I knew down deep that something had to change or I wasn't going to be able to fulfill the calling God had placed on my life. So on January 1, 2002, I began to get up two hours earlier than usual to spend concentrated time in the Word each day.

January 1, 2002, through June 19, 2005, was a time of exponential spiritual growth in my life. My memories of those morning quiet times with the Lord are so sweet. I remember lingering over His Word. Hungering for it more and more each day. Seeing for the first time the great worth of my salvation even though I had been saved for many years.

But why, you might ask, did I place an ending date on this time of great spiritual growth?

Friends, I'm going to share a secret with you that I pray will help you find peace and freedom. Because if you have experienced this, you'll know you are NOT ALONE.

June 19, 2005, was the day I experienced bringing a new life into the world for the first time. It was also the day that my nectar-sweet alone time in the Word of God came to a crashing halt.

Babies and Quiet Time?!

I was unprepared for the emotions I would experience as a new mom. Despite having a master's in counseling and knowing I might struggle, I was still unprepared. The first year of my sweet baby boy's life was filled with doubt, and I found myself regularly entertaining thoughts like these:

"Who am I now?"

"I'm totally responsible for keeping this baby alive. There's never going to be a vacation from this child."

"Why won't You help me with this, Lord? Why won't You make him sleep? Why won't You make breast-feeding beautiful and easy? I can't even feed my own child without a fight!"

"Why are You doing this to me, God?"

"I'M A FAILURE."

The first six months after he was born, my husband and I didn't even have a church home, so I had no "Titus 2" women to help me through my fears and anxieties as a new mother. I fell into the baby blues, a form of depression. And instead of choosing to turn to the Lord with my fears, I got angry with Him, thought He had deserted me, thought that if He really loved me, He would change my circumstances.

When we finally committed to a new church home, I realized I was in desperate need for fellowship with other women, so I began attending the women's Bible studies and eventually leading them again, something I dearly love to do. I came out of the fog, one small step at a time.

I knew something had to change or I wasn't going to be able to fulfill the calling God had placed on my life. I began to see again—see His great love for me, see that He had been there all along, was with me every long night, every stress-filled day, every battle—He was there. I found Him again in His Word, and I was finally able to stop living based on what *had been* in my life and instead, live for what He was doing now.

Another One?

When my second son was born just twenty-three short months later, I found myself tempted to respond the exact same way. It didn't get any easier, but I never wanted to feel so far away from my God again. And thanks to Him, I learned some interesting things . . .

Quiet time doesn't have to be in the morning. God doesn't care for legalism, but there is something particularly anointed about rising early to start your day in the Word, hiding the Word of God in your heart so that you might not sin against Him throughout the day.

Get creative! I think God delights in our creativity when it comes to time alone with Him each day. When my sons were

31

very young, they both went through seasons of chronic ear infections until finally getting tubes. During those times, both about five months long, my husband and I didn't sleep. At. All. Add to that shift-work and Mama working (at that time) four days a week and you get an equation for disaster. I simply could not force myself to get up one millisecond before I absolutely had to in the morning, and I often fell asleep at my desk during lunch. The only time I consistently had to hear from the Word of God was on my drive to and from work and (prepare yourself, I'm going to be blunt here) when I was pumping milk for my children while at work.

I bought the ESV (my favorite) New Testament on CD and would listen to a few chapters from the Word on the drive to and from work. Then, for about twenty minutes, two times a day, I would hole up in an office without windows, "hook up," and open up my Bible to those same verses I had listened to on the way in that morning. I was doing my best to fill my heart and head with the Word of God, study it in-depth, and stay close to the One who would give me the strength to get through a difficult time.

Just read a little. Also during that time, a friend of mine, a pastor's wife with three daughters very close together, shared with me that she had struggled to find consistent time in the Word each day as a young mother. Her secret? A psalm and a proverb a day. That's it. It sustained her until such a time that her family life could allow her to set aside more time. I immediately incorporated that into my own routine.

Make the Word available everywhere. I once heard a story about Reverend Billy Graham. I have no idea if it's true, but it's a fantastic idea, so I'll share it with you. Apparently, the reverend took the call to feast on the Word at all times seriously and was known to keep several copies of the Bible laying around his home, so that anytime he entered a new room he could read a few verses and meditate on them while performing day-to-day activities. What brilliance! And what an easy way for young mothers or working mothers with little time to themselves to spend time in the Word.

Quiet Time Is a Must for the Weary Mama

Time in the Word of God and communion with Him is essential to living a full, joyful, hope-filled life as a Christian. More than that, it's essential to our ability to hear from the Lord. We've been promised trouble (John 16:33) in this world simply because we're Christians. Life is hard. Being a parent is hard. There are times when I long for the selfishness of my single life—when it was all about what was best for me—but this season of difficulty has kept me diving headfirst to the cross.

No matter what it costs, no matter what it looks like, I know I must have more and more of Him. And I want to encourage you to commit now to joyfully setting aside time each day to spend with the One who gives you your life and breath and being. Feeling God's presence and gaining confidence in your ability to hear from Him depends on it.

Believing God

Certainly the hardest of the four parts of prayer, believing God, is easier for many of us when we're young and haven't experienced much of life.

In late 2011 I had my first miscarriage. It was the tail end of around seven years of loss among my family and friends and was probably the proverbial straw that broke the camel's back. I wrote about the process of grief I went through in *Hope for the Weary Mom: Where God Meets You in Your Mess*, so I won't duplicate it here, but I just need to get this out on the table:

It's hard to believe God . . .

when you've prayed for a miracle for over fifteen years and haven't gotten it.

when you've asked God for healing and lost a loved one instead.

when you've prayed for God to protect your sons and it seems like He hasn't.

Yes, God doesn't always work on our schedule, or work according to our plans. We pray in accordance with what we believe to be His heart, and we believe His promises are true, but when life throws a curve ball (or worse, a sucker punch) our way, it can be difficult to regain the ease with which we used to believe in miracles.

In his book *A Praying Life*, Paul Miller says, "Strong Christians do pray more, but they pray more because they realize how weak they are. They don't try to hide it from themselves. Weakness is a channel that allows them to access grace."[2] After an intense season of loss, I can confidently say these words are true. I know I'm weak. Just this morning as I prayed again about a weak area in my life, it occurred to me I'm not sure I have the willpower to make the necessary changes so I can be victorious over it. At first, that realization made me sad, but then another thought crept in.

Remember the story of the little boy in Matthew 14 who offered his five loaves of bread and two fish to Jesus?

> Then he ordered the crowds to sit down on the grass, and taking the five loaves and the two fish, he looked up to heaven and said a blessing. Then he broke the loaves and gave them to the disciples, and the disciples gave them to the crowds. And they all ate and were satisfied. And they took up twelve baskets full of the broken pieces left over.
>
> Matthew 14:19–20

2. Paul Miller, *A Praying Life* (Colorado Springs: NavPress, 2009), 56.

This precious little boy (yes, it was a *boy* who did something generous, kind, and thoughtful; it does happen every once in a while!) gave Jesus everything he had. And even though what he had was so very small, Jesus took it and turned it into something overflowing with bounty.

Just a little faith can move mountains. Even Samson's parents, desperate for God to show them how to raise their son, believed in the God who "works wonders" (Judges 13:19). I think their devotion and simple faith beg this question: If we were to get serious about praying for our sons, what could God do? The possibilities are endless.

If we fasted, cried out for days, begged God for answers, laid on hands, anointed with oil—all the things the Bible tells us to do either with specific direction or by example of the biblical characters we know and love—what would happen?

I think we'd change the world.

Mark Batterson, in *Praying Circles Around Your Children*, says, "Call me a simpleton, but I believe that if we simply do what the people in the Bible did, we may experience what they experienced."[3] I'm not saying that each and every biblical occurrence will be duplicated for us today, but it stands to reason that if we simply believe what the Bible says, and *do it*, God will honor our hearts somehow, someday, even if it's just with the joy of walking in obedience to Him and having a pure heart before Him.

Note: It's Not About Us

When God decided to bless Manoah and his wife with a child after years of barrenness, it wasn't totally for them. Yes, it blessed them. Yes, it answered a cry of their hearts for a child, but it

3. Mark Batterson, *Praying Circles Around Your Children* (Grand Rapids, MI: Zondervan, 2012), 79.

really wasn't about them. It was about Him. It was about saving Israel. It was about God getting all the glory from someone's life.

Manoah begged God for answers. He was a man of action. So was King Solomon (David's son). When told he could ask God for anything, Solomon asked for wisdom (1 Kings 3:7–9). *Matthew Henry's Commentary on the Whole Bible* has this to say about him: "Solomon enquire[d] concerning the good men should *do*, not the good they should *have*" (emphasis mine).

Are our prayers more focused on what we want our sons to have, on how changes in their behavior will benefit us, or on what we need to do to help them grow into godly men? Scripture is full of verses that tell us God sees and draws near to people with humble hearts. If we're not just looking for God to make our lives easier, but truly want Him to teach us to raise godly sons, He will answer in His own time. When He does, friends, it'll be a whole lot less about answering our prayers and a whole lot more about fulfilling His purpose for the lives He creates.

Give Jesus what faith you have, mamas. He specializes in taking nothing and turning it into something.

"It's me again, Lord. I just need to confess to You that believing You see me, or hear me, or even that You want to bless me is sometimes very hard. I wish I could see the way You do instead of being so limited by my humanness. But You've asked me to trust You, and I want to. Help me? O Lord, I do believe. Help my unbelief!" (Mark 9:24).

Going It Alone

Note: There's a whole population of moms out there who could be called "spiritually single." They're married, perhaps to good men, but are in the fight to raise godly sons alone. Having an unbelieving husband can be at least as difficult as not having a husband at all, and depending on the circumstances, maybe worse. This chapter is based on the life of my grandmother, who raised three boys (and one girl) alone, but I think much of her story applies to spiritually single moms too. The story of Timothy from the Bible always encourages me when I think of moms going it alone. His father was an unbeliever, but the prayers and instruction of his mother and grandmother paved the way for him to come to Jesus. Praise God for His tendency to take our earthly lack and make it into something beautiful for His glory. I'm praying for you and believing God to do this in the life of your son.

She was abandoned by her first husband and left with three hungry boy-mouths to feed. Alone in the late 1930s, she returned home to a place where she would face the judging eyes of people who didn't understand divorce. Forced by a choice she never wanted to make, she returned to her parents' home because she couldn't feed her own children now that he was gone.

By the time I was born, my paternal grandmother had survived that early tragedy and was even thriving in life, but I know she remembered. A thing like that changes a person, becomes part of the fabric of their response to life—always feeling the loss, working hard to stay ahead so that everyone has what they need. But she desperately loved her children and was determined to teach her boys to be good men. In doing so, she somehow managed to raise men who chose a different path from the one shown them by their father. All three contributed to their communities, worked hard at everything they did, and became learned men, wise men, and family men by deliberate choice, not because they were taught by the man who was supposed to be their role model.

Even though I'm not a single mom raising my boys alone, I know what it is to have days when you want to throw your hands in the air and . . . Just. Give. Up. The financial costs of raising children alone are staggering. But you, my friend, make decisions every day that go way beyond money. My hat is off to single moms who desire to raise their boys well, and I have faith that God sees you and loves you no matter where you are or what you've been through.

Many of you have written to us since our online community for mothers of boys, the MOB Society, was launched, asking for specific tips and tools for single moms trying to raise godly men alone, and I knew it needed to be a chapter in this book. But honestly, I wasn't raised by a single mom. My father had a profoundly positive impact on my life, as did my mom, so I wasn't sure what I would share with you.

I looked around my life and tried to find an example of a mom, single or not, who did a better job of raising boys than my own grandmother, and I just couldn't find one. Her story fills me with faith, knowing that if she could do it in a time when life was so much harder, I can do it now. So can you.

I think she would've liked knowing that her struggles and absolute determination to raise good men could serve to help other moms.

This chapter is dedicated to her, and to you, but please don't make it into a formula for success. There aren't any surefire formulas when it comes to raising children. If there were, all of our children would end up perfect. Since that's obviously not the way it works, please don't be tempted to make these into an A + B = Good, God-Fearing Men equation. Instead, as you read, just ask the Lord to lead you, and allow the Holy Spirit to touch your heart and show you where you could make adjustments. Be inspired to be the best mom you can be. That'll be enough.

Good Men

Cack, as we called her, died when I was just sixteen, and nearly every day since becoming a mom I've wished for time with her to talk about raising good men. My husband is highly involved in parenting our sons. He's with them every day; I don't think they even comprehend what it means for a dad to abandon his family. But raising boys is still hard. Much more so when a mom is doing it alone.

How do you teach them what a devoted father looks like when their father's not around?

How do you teach them how a husband treats his wife, when you're trying to be both mother and father?

How do you raise up a generation of men who stay, who persevere, when all they've seen is a man who walked away?

Over the years, Cack's three sons stood together, fought for each other, walked through devastating life events together, and rescued each other. Opinionated at best, and stubborn to a fault, each one of them chose something different for his family than he was dealt by their father. In doing so, they became something very special—three men determined to do things the right way, determined that their children would not suffer the way they had, determined that their children would not be without fathers, determined that their children's lives would be easier than theirs had been, determined that their families would never question whether they were loved.

In preparation for writing this chapter, I asked my dad to write down some of his memories of his mom and share what it was that made her so successful in her life's mission. I wanted to know, for your sake and mine, exactly what she did to raise three boys on her own, boys who didn't turn into statistics, who loved their mama desperately, and who didn't leave their families.

Here are a few of the examples he shared. . . .

Sacrifice

Soon after she moved in with her parents, Cack began looking for a job to help provide the basics for her children. Never comfortable with allowing someone else to pay her children's way in life, she started out with a part-time job for a local lawyer, and within a few months was working full time as a secretary. In the 1930s there was no Internet, of course, no make-money-from-home opportunities she knew of or could invite into her parents' home. So her choice, if she wanted to provide for her sons, was to work outside the home.

And I wonder what it cost her? Time away from her sons, missing the everyday moments all of the other mothers at home with their children were getting, baking cookies before they got home from school, and on and on. So many lost moments and experiences that required a simple faith in God, her parents, and even her community to care for the parts of her boys' lives she couldn't because she was working to provide for them.

I interviewed some single moms on the MOB Society Facebook page about what it cost them to be a single, working mom. This is what they said:

"The cost is astronomical."—Ashley

"Time and money . . . at times, sanity, as well."—Jennifer

"When I have to work overtime (meaning I have no choice, either that or lose my job), it's twelve- and sixteen-hour days. I don't even see my boys on sixteen-hour days."—Misty

"Nana and the baby-sitters know more about my boys than I often do. I find I'm missing out on a lot of firsts."—Katie

"I would do whatever it takes to make sure they are taken care of. If it weren't for the help of family and friends, I'd hate to think of where we'd be."—Tina

"Being a single mom and working out of the home is SO very expensive in dollars and time away from my son."—Michelle

"It is not the life I thought I'd have, but God has taken care of us. The emotional costs are the highest for me."—Tina

"The weight of the responsibility of doing it alone is overwhelming."—Mary

"Our hectic lifestyle and time apart are my biggest regrets as a single mom."—Anne

"I am blessed more than most in my situation. But . . . sometimes it just stinks."—Kimberly

"I would love nothing more than to be home for my son and have a more 'perfect' atmosphere. But honestly, if you focus and are selfless with your time, you can still be a great mother and have a full-time job."—Deb

When other moms could clean while their children were at school, my grandmother had to keep her home around her work schedule. While other moms gathered together for downtime or playdates, she took extra hours at the office to pay for band instruments or football pads. While married moms simply asked their husbands for enough money for groceries, she had to beg hers to remember child support just to buy her sons shoes.

The only thing my dad ever remembers his mom doing purely for her own pleasure outside of their home was playing bridge, which she did years after her divorce, when her sons were a little older and functioning more independently. She also often played the piano to relax and unwind. Aside from those two hobbies, everything my grandmother did, every choice she made, was for the benefit of her children.

I look at my own life and I see many opportunities afforded me because of a hardworking, loving husband. I work about thirty hours a week as a writer, blogger, and entrepreneur from my home. But I get to do the work I *want* to do, or feel called to do, not what I *have* to do to make ends meet. It's different.

My grandmother was a truly selfless woman; nothing was more important to her than her children's health and well-being. They saw that in her and respected her deeply for it. It exuded from within her and was clearly visible to everyone she encountered because of the choices she made and the way she lived her life. She had the hearts of her sons until the day she died, and I think one of the ways she made that happen was by laying down her life for theirs.

The one quality about my grandmother that leaves a lasting impression on me was the relationship she had with her sons. They weren't perfect—neither was she—but she had their hearts. They loved her, respected her, and took care of her. None of them moved more than an hour away from her. They fixed her house, changed the oil in her car, wrote to her faithfully when serving in the military overseas, and protected her until she slipped from this life into eternity.

That kind of devotion comes from years of hard-won respect and plain hard work. Even though it might not seem like he really sees, there's much to be said for a child who watches his mother give her all on his behalf.

I'm not advocating for placing our children's needs above our relationship with God. I'm not encouraging us to place our children on a pedestal, and I'm not making a case for catering to their every whim. But what will we sacrifice so our boys can have the best life we can possibly give them? Will we trade a night out with friends so we can have a night in to hear our boys' hearts and just play with them? Will we forsake new clothes so our boys can play in the band? Will we learn how to sew to make our clothes last longer? Will we burn the midnight oil in prayer for our sons, asking God to protect them, lead them, grab hold of their hearts?

Are there some changes we can make to give our children a greater place of priority in our lives? Every one of us reading this (and writing it . . . ahem) can say yes, and they're probably coming to mind even as you read this. Our hearts have a way of knowing what we really need to do. The trick is just to do it. If you don't know what you need to sacrifice, pray and ask God to gently remove anything that doesn't bring glory to Him during this season of your life.

Or maybe you're a mom who knows down in her knower she's already living the sacrificial life for her sons. Well done, mama. I believe your hard work will pay off in the end, and your sons will rise up and call you blessed one day very soon.

I'm challenged by the way my grandmother loved her boys, and it blesses me to know I come from a long line of women willing to make the sacrifice and fight for the hearts of their sons.

Ask for Help

When Cack could no longer pay the bills or afford doctor visits for her children, and her repeated efforts to save her marriage and get her husband to contribute to the family needs failed, Cack knew she needed help. The year before she moved home, my father had pneumonia three times, and it was just too much for her to handle alone.

So she moved back in with her parents.

My great-grandfather was something of a stern man who expected nothing less than respect and obedience. I've heard hilarious stories of life in their home with three crazy, wild boys. Dinners were served and eaten in complete silence (can you even imagine?), and the penalty for disobedience was hours spent standing still on the fireplace stoop.

My great-grandmother was a crackerjack herself, always making the boys behave and raising the bar high for what she considered acceptable behavior. I'm sure the dynamic wasn't perfect, but having a stable home life with a male figure to look up to was a wonderful provision in the lives of my dad and his two brothers.

Cack's parents gave her a roof over her head and help raising her children when she needed them most, but I imagine it was hard for her to go back home.

Asking for help always requires humility and a teachable spirit. Even though I have amazing parents, I can't imagine moving back in with them now that I've established my own household. Why? Because I don't have exactly the same family dynamic they do. My husband and I do things a little differently than they did. Our likes and dislikes are different, and it's hard to have two people ruling the same roost. I'm sure there were plenty of times my grandmother longed for her own home, but she humbled herself for the sake of her sons. Turns out that one decision to bring a father-figure into their lives was one of the best things she could have done.

Every boy needs someone to teach him how to be a man. Most often that person is his father, but when there's no father to take on that job, or even if the father is there but *won't* take on the role, a substitute will do.

I worked for many years serving women in crisis pregnancies through the ministry of my local crisis pregnancy center. During that time, one of our faithful volunteers lost her husband to cancer. It was a miraculous time for her as she watched her prayers come to fruition in her husband's near-deathbed profession of faith. She glowed with the grace of God at his funeral and proudly proclaimed that her God had met all of her needs according to His riches in Christ Jesus (Philippians 4:19). But with four children to care for, two of them twin boys, she soon found herself in a position of needing to find someone to be an example for her boys.

When I heard my boss offer to spend time mentoring her sons, I knew I had witnessed something profound and good, and it made me wonder why more godly men don't offer to do the same. What a difference they could make in the lives of boys by sacrificing a bit of their time each week.

My dad was always there for my brother and me when we needed him. In fact, I can't remember a time when I needed him that he didn't find a way to get to me. When my mom was working toward her master's degree, we spent many a night huddled up in a corner of our small-town restaurant talking about life and doing math problems on paper napkins. He spent hours of time with me at the kitchen table helping me figure out chemistry and math problems that came easily to his engineer's mind and hard to my writer's mind.

But he wasn't just there for me. He also served as a listening ear for his nieces and nephews, encouraging them to follow their dreams, work hard, and contribute something to the world.

Is there a man in your church or community who could serve as a mentor for your boys? Someone they can look up to? Spend time with? Ask questions they might be embarrassed to ask their moms? If so, humble yourself and go ask for help. Don't wait for him to come to you like my boss did for the volunteer who lost her husband. That may or may not happen for you. Be proactive in fighting for the heart of your son, and work hard to provide him with godly examples. Pray and ask God to send you the right person in the right time. If you need to, make sacrifices to be near someone who can help grow your son in the right ways, helping him to follow Christ and become a good man.

Help Them Dream

It was years ago when my dad and I drove through the campus of Virginia Tech. The big, strong man I trusted more than any other man loved to show me where he had gone to college and help me dream about the time I would attend school there.

"That was where my dorm room was, Brooke. Right over there.

"This building is where I had most of my math classes, and this one was where the English department was back then. I didn't like that building.

"Here's the building where your uncle played a prank on us. . . .

"When you get older and go to college here, you're going to have so much fun, just like I did. You'll work hard, but I know you'll have great memories just like mine."

My little brown eyes gazed in wonder at the big, beautiful campus. And even though it scared me a little to think about a time when I would be away from my parents, I never even once questioned whether or not I would go to college. Truthfully, it never entered my mind *not* to go to college. I believe it was because my father helped me dream and expanded my mind to be able to think beyond its limits.

Dad worked deliberately and sometimes painstakingly to help my brother and me dream. He got it honestly—his own mother had done the same for him. Even though she didn't have enough money to pay for him to go to college, she told him he would. And as they passed by the local factory that supported much of the county in jobs, she said to him, "You might work there one day, but not as a factory worker. . . . I want you to manage it."

She knew there was nothing wrong with being a factory worker. She just wanted him to dream beyond what he could see . . . beyond what he thought he could achieve on his own. And so even though he had to work his own way through college at Virginia Tech—going to school for a quarter, then working a quarter, going to school for a quarter, then working a quarter, etc.—and even though it took him eight years to get a four-year degree because he had to pay for it himself, when my father retired from that local factory, he held a top managerial position right under the plant manager.

Cack encouraged her boys to dream, and so my father encouraged me to dream. It's a trait I will work hard to pass on to my own boys—to dream God's dreams for their lives.

Are you helping your son dream about the bigger vision God has for his life? Do you look at life for what it is, or what it can be? Do you call out the gifts in your son's life, helping him to grow into his God-given passions and callings? Even if your son is quite young, you can help him see the big picture—let him know he can do anything God wants him to do, be anything God wants him to be. You can encourage him to fight for those who are too weak to fight for themselves. Does he see you caring about your neighbors and those in your community who need help? Does he know about the people all over the world whose trials and struggles are so much worse than his own?

Give him a new perspective on life. Help him dream God's dreams for his life. Tell him about the needs of this world so his heart has the chance to solve them. Call out the gifts within him and watch him reach, stretch, and then soar.

And So . . .

If raising boys in a two-parent home is hard, going it alone is just that much harder. But I believe there are some important lessons to learn from my grandmother's story and countless other single moms like her.

1. Life won't be perfect—don't expect it to be—but do set the bar high for excellence in your life and in your son's life. Expect him to live up to it.

In a letter I recently read written by my grandmother to her ex-in-laws after the early death of their son (her ex-husband, my father's father), she stated, "Thank you for your interest in the boys. I'm sure they will prove themselves worthy of it." The irony is that her ex-in-laws, my father's grandparents, never really showed much interest in the boys at all. They struggled with their son's issues his whole life, trying to get him help to overcome alcoholism. But they rarely reached out to his sons. The one time they showed any interest in their grandsons, my grandmother assured them of what she knew: they were worth any sacrifice that had to be made on their behalf. She lived with a firm confidence in her sons' abilities to do the right thing, and she modeled doing the next right thing for them over and over again. They might not have had a father who was a good man, or did the right things, but their mother did, and she surrounded them with other people who did too.

2. Do whatever it takes to protect your children.

After barely surviving for over a year with three boys in her own home, trying hard to get her husband to take care of his family and failing, and not even having the money to take her children to the doctor when they were sick, my grandmother knew she had to make a choice. She could've taken the easy route, held on to her pride, and forced them to live in poverty, but she didn't. She humbled herself, asked for help, and moved back into her parents' home for a season.

Raising good men may require you to live a life you never thought you could. You may find yourself learning to sew your own clothes, moving away from bad influences, becoming a coupon expert, or even moving in with family . . . doing whatever it takes.

3. Pray.

Never underestimate the power of God at work in the hearts of your sons. In *Hope for the Weary Mom*, I offered a challenge to mamas whose knees are worn out from the hard-parenting prayers. I like to call it the Weary Mom Manifesto. If you believe it, will you pray it with me?

"I will never give up on my family. And I will never give up on God's ability to work in their hearts."

Remember, "Because he bends down to listen, I will pray as long as I have breath!" (Psalm 116:2 NLT).

How to Use This Book

When I first began writing about praying for boys, it became clear to me that many moms needed help knowing how to get started. In truth, when I first felt the call to go deeper in my own prayer life, I wasn't really sure what to say beyond the simple "Help them, Lord" prayers I raised every day. I only knew that God had called me to be a prayer warrior on behalf of my sons, and that alone was enough to make me start thinking and looking for a better way to pray.

The only logical place I knew to turn was to the Bible. If the Bible is God's Word—something I believe with all my heart—and if it is so fully true that we can build our lives on and around it, and if, as the Bible itself claims, God's Word doesn't return void but does what it sets out to do (Isaiah 55:11), it seemed logical to pray God's Word back to Him for my boys, asking Him to accomplish it in their lives.

That's the foundation for this book—that God's Word is true and powerful and a perfect guide for parents who long to battle for the hearts of their sons in prayer.

You might look at this book and see it as a wonderful resource. Great! I hope you do! But the last thing I want you to do is skim through it and then put it on your shelf to collect dust because you don't know how to use it. This book was written with three main purposes in mind: to encourage parents to pray for their sons, to teach them how to do it, and to inspire them to keep doing it on a regular basis by explaining why it's a vital part of raising godly men. Below are a few ways I envision parents using *Praying for Boys* on an ongoing basis. Feel free to use any of them exactly as they are written, or just use them as inspiration to build your own plan.

Ideas for Praying for Your Boy

1. Gather a group of like-minded parents together and use the guide at the end of the book to start a 21 Days of Prayer for Sons challenge in your home, church, school, or community. There's power and encouragement to be found in joining with other prayer warriors.

2. Pray "The Things They Need Most" prayers that follow. You'll find ten prayers in each chapter listed after a brief discussion of a specific topic. You can pray them all in the morning before your boy gets up, a few here and there throughout the day, or together as a family before bed.

3. I have had success (and fun) praying on the hours. I set the alarm on my phone to go off each hour between 9:00 a.m. and 7:00 p.m. and pray one of the ten prayers each hour.

4. Consider choosing three topics to pray through each month for just over nine months. For example, pray a different prayer listed in the "Heart Change" chapter each day for ten days. Then pray a different prayer listed in the "Obedience" chapter each day for ten days. Then pray a different prayer listed in the "Overcoming Fears" chapter each day for ten days. This provides you with a slow, deliberate method for

praying your way through the material. At the end of the nine to ten months, take a break and then start over in the new year! This may also be a good time to study the topics of prayer with your son more in-depth. For character-training resources to use with your children, check out the ministry of Doorposts (www.doorposts.com).

5. For an even more in-depth way to pray the topics over your son, consider praying through one topic per month over and over again. This will take almost two years to complete, but at the end of that time you'll be a pro prayer warrior!

6. As you pray through the topics, highlight those that really speak to you or seem to target an area your son is struggling with. Craft them into one longer prayer to pray over him every day for the next month. To learn more about how I do this, check out the *Praying for Boys* resource page at www.prayingforboys.com/resources. I've created a guide to help you learn how to craft Scripture prayers yourself!

However you end up using this book, I invite you to commit in your heart right now to continue praying for your son. It's the part of the battle for his heart most overlooked in our culture today, but in truth, there couldn't be anything more important.

Before we start praying, can I tell you one more thing?

God is FOR you.

This parenting of the male species is hard—whether you have an adventurous boy, a scholarly boy, a rambunctious boy, or a bookworm boy. A little boy, married boy, big boy, or somewhere-in-between boy. Sinner boy, saved boy, sanctified boy.

It's still hard.

I've watched your words, you boy-mamas, as you've emailed me, commented on the MOB Society blog, or chatted with me over coffee, and I confess: I've been totally overwhelmed for you . . . for me. I've rested my head many nights, speechless that God would allow me to kneel with you and pray for His hand in our boys' lives.

Several times I've asked God, "What are You doing?" And other times I've read about a mom's deep burden for her son and all I could utter was, "Oh, God."

He hears our groanings.

The coupled pain and hope that keeps a mama on her knees wears a carpet thin. But He hears you, and He is for you.

You are the apple of His eye. His beloved. His thoughts toward you are many and His plans for you are good. He will never leave you nor forsake you.

When your son takes his first steps and you realize for the first time your baby is growing up . . . God is for you.

When you give it your all and his heart doesn't change . . . God is for you.

When you wake up and he's five (or nine or sixteen) and you realize there are already so many moments you've missed and will never get back . . . God is for you.

When you realize the home life you desperately wanted to provide for him may never happen . . . God is for you.

When you realize how your own sinful choices have affected him . . . God is for you.

When you're defeated and ready to quit . . . God is for you.

When you see the desires of his heart and realize they're not always good . . . God is for you.

When your son gets hurt, or that heartache you always wanted to protect him from happens . . . God is for you.

When his heart doesn't belong to just you anymore . . . God is for you.

When he makes choices that hurt you . . . God is for you.

When the threads of your carpet are worn bare from the praying, begging, hoping in God to complete the work He started . . . God is for you.

And His heart for you is good.

Remember that? Now, let's start praying.

The Things They Need Most

Heart Change

I will give you a new heart, and a new spirit I will put within you. And I will remove the heart of stone from your flesh and give you a heart of flesh. And I will put my Spirit within you, and cause you to walk in my statutes and be careful to obey my rules.

Ezekiel 36:26–27

Young boys are just a whole different breed. Mothers of girls often glare at me as if to say, *"Do they act that way all the time?"* I want to glare right back and say, "Yes! They do!"

Parenting my sons is my greatest joy and my greatest challenge. I love them to the ends of the earth and back, but honestly, sometimes they suck the life out of me. Each day I target their hearts, aiming high and taking my best shot, but so many days I fall short, or my aim is off, or I'm just too weary to pull the bow back far enough for the arrow to have the strength to pierce the heart. I go to bed those nights exhausted physically and emotionally. But in my weakness, God is strong.

Perhaps the best place for a weary mom to be is exhausted and on her knees.

With each day that passes, I'm more convinced I have absolutely no power to change the hearts of my boys. Oh, I can change their behavior if I try hard enough. Anyone can do that. But I know that what's in the heart eventually comes out. I know if their knees are ever to bend to Jesus as Savior, their hearts must bend first.

And that's God's business.

I'm praying you'll grasp this concept so clearly it will bring you strength and peace in the midst of your wildest storms. You cannot change the heart of your boy. You can't. Period. It's not your job. It's so important you get this, friend, because you're going to want to be able to change his heart more than anything in the world. Days, months, maybe even years of endless toil and labor for the sake of your son will go by with no apparent fruit. Night after night you will cry out to the Lord for change. Day after day you will parent intentionally, seeking the heart of your son. But until the King of Kings and Lord of Lords turns your son's heart of stone to a heart of flesh, his actions will be motivated by what is pleasing to himself rather than by what is pleasing to the Lord.

As we journey into this process of praying for our sons, let's remember this foundational concept: The first and most important action we must take is to pray that God will change their hearts of stone to hearts of flesh. Ezekiel 36:26–27 has become the theme of my parenting. I pray these verses for my sons most every day because I know that until their hearts are softened by the Lord, to the Lord, nothing else matters all that much.

PRAYERS FOR HEART CHANGE

Give _____ a new heart and a new spirit put within him. Remove the heart of stone from his flesh and give him a heart of flesh (Ezekiel 36:26).

May _____ honor You, God, with his heart, and not just his lips (Isaiah 29:13).

May _____ out of the good treasure of his heart produce good, for out of the abundance of his heart his mouth speaks (Luke 6:45).

May _____'s heart cry be, "Not my will, but Yours, be done" (Luke 22:42).

May _____ draw near to You, Lord, for You promise to draw near to him. May he cleanse his hands and purify his heart (James 4:8).

Create in _____ a clean heart, O God, and renew a right spirit within him (Psalm 51:10).

May _____ first clean the inside of the cup and the plate, that the outside also may be clean (Matthew 23:26).

May _____ be like the wise man, whose heart inclines him to the right (Ecclesiastes 10:2).

May _____ not take idols into his heart, and set the stumbling block of his iniquity before his face (Ezekiel 14:3).

When _____ hears Your Word, Lord, may he be cut to the heart (Acts 2:37).

For Reflection or Discussion

1. This chapter starts with some impressions of how mothers of girls respond around boys. What differences between boys and girls have you seen or experienced?

2. Have you ever found yourself physically and emotionally exhausted from parenting your son? How have you handled it in the past?

3. As mentioned in this chapter, "What's in the heart eventually comes out. I know if their knees are ever to bend to Jesus as Savior, their hearts must bend first. And that's God's business." Have you given much thought to what God expects of you as a parent, versus the areas that are really more His job? Make a list below of your job responsibilities as a parent, and compare it with those God says are His job.

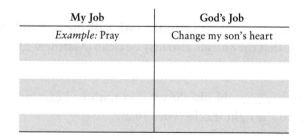

My Job	God's Job
Example: Pray	Change my son's heart

4. Consider your own parenting style. Is the way you interact with your son targeting his heart and motivating him toward real heart-change, or do you mainly focus on changing behavior?

5. Jesus called the Pharisees "whitewashed tombs" (Matthew 23:27) because they only cared about how they appeared on the outside, and not about cleaning up their hearts. How does this apply to the way we need to raise our sons?

Obedience

Children, obey your parents in the Lord . . .

Ephesians 6:1

"Son," I said to the droopy-eyed little boy standing in front of me, "what did you do wrong?"

Feet shuffled, hands crossed, and impatient legs squirmed around with the discomfort of being caught. He looked up at me and said, "I didn't obey."

The Importance of Obedience

When my sons were very little, we intentionally started using the word *obey* to make it a part of their vocabulary, even before they could truly understand its meaning. We decided not to use phrases like "Mind your mommy!" or "Do what I say!" because we wanted to train our sons to think in biblical language. Believe me, it didn't take long for them to understand what *obey* meant.

62

There's great debate over when parents should begin disciplining their children, but to us the decision was easy. When the child begins to deliberately disobey, he or she should be disciplined. This earth-shattering moment, when Mommy's angel looks up with malicious intent and screams "NO!" is easy to recognize as disobedience. Every mom knows when that moment comes. That's why the word *obey* is so important in parenting. As Ephesians 6:1–3 says:

> Children, obey your parents in the Lord, for this is right. "Honor your father and mother" (this is the first commandment with a promise), "that it may go well with you and that you may live long in the land."

Moms (and dads), we MUST teach our sons to obey us, even if it takes years of loving consistency to see their hearts respond to our teaching. Obedience and submission to authority are normal parts of life. For the rest of their days, our sons will have to submit to someone or something. Even if your son becomes the CEO of the biggest, most powerful company (or country) in the world, he will still have to answer to his Maker. Training him now to respect and submit to authority sets him up for success of the greatest kind.

Why Obedience Is Important for Boys

Before we were married, my husband and I attended a conference together on the topic of biblical relationships. During the session on selecting a mate, the speaker said something I will never forget:

"Ladies, if your man cannot submit to Jesus, he cannot lead you. A man must be willing to be led before he can truly lead."[1]

1. Tommy Nelson, Song of Solomon conference.

Life-changing words.

Training our sons to obey their parents is not an option. Scripture is full of warnings for parents and children alike who neglect this important detail. And in the teaching of obedience lies one of the most glorious opportunities to prove the gospel message to our sons.

It goes something like this:

"Son, you're right. You didn't obey Mommy. God says you must obey Mommy and Daddy, doesn't He? It's hard to obey, isn't it? Everything in you wants your own way! It's fun to hit your brother sometimes. It's fun to be too loud, and sometimes it makes you feel good about yourself to tell Mommy no. But God, who made you, says you must obey. You can't do it by yourself, can you? No matter how hard you try to be good and obey Mommy, you just can't get it right all the time. That's why we love God so much, son! God knew you couldn't do it by yourself! He knew you would choose to sin instead of obey! He knew you would need help! So He sent His only Son, Jesus, to die for your sins and take the punishment you deserved. Then God raised Jesus from the dead, and now Jesus is with God in heaven, just waiting for you to confess your sin and ask Him to help you fight the sin in your heart! Isn't that great news? We need Jesus! Let's pray now and ask Jesus to help you!"

Of course, when and how you share this message will depend on the age and maturity of your son. But it's easy to see how teaching our boys to obey leads naturally to the gospel message. If our boys never learn the importance of obeying and never see their inability to obey by their own power, how will they ever recognize their need for a Savior?

So let's pray for the hearts of our sons to grasp the need to obey. And while we're at it, let's pray the Lord renews our vision and ability to teach them this vital lesson by increasing our desire to obey Him.

PRAYERS FOR OBEDIENCE

Whether it is favorable or unfavorable, may _____ obey You so that it will go well with him (Jeremiah 42:6).

May _____ obey his parents in You, Lord, for this is right (Ephesians 6:1).

May _____ obey his leaders and submit to them, for they are keeping watch over his soul, as those who will have to give an account.

Let _____ do this with joy and not with groaning (Hebrews 13:17).

May _____ obey You rather than men (Acts 5:29).

May _____ return to You, Lord, his God, and obey with all his heart and all his soul all the commands You have given (Deuteronomy 30:2).

May _____ walk after You, God, and fear You and keep Your commandments and obey Your voice. May he serve You and hold fast to You (Deuteronomy 13:4).

May _____ stop his sinning and begin to obey You, Lord, his God (Jeremiah 26:13).

May _____ obey Your commandments and remain in Your love (John 15:10).

May _____ show his love for You, Christ, by obeying Your commands (John 14:15).

May we be full of joy at _____'s obedience (Romans 16:19).

For Reflection or Discussion

1. Describe the first time your son deliberately disobeyed you. Did you recognize it immediately? How did it make you feel? Parents of older boys: How has the battle for obedience changed as your boy has gotten older? Describe some victories and failures in this area.

2. Do you have a plan for teaching your son obedience? Or are you more of a "heat of the moment" kind of parent?

3. Have you ever considered how teaching obedience leads naturally to a deeper understanding of the gospel?

4. This chapter included this statement: "Ladies, if your man cannot submit to Jesus, he cannot lead you. A man must be willing to be led before he can truly lead." How does this idea affect your thoughts about teaching your son obedience?

5. Are there any discipline practices you've been using that need to be tweaked in order to better reflect the gospel message?

Overcoming Fears

Once I became a Christian, I came to realize that Jesus my Savior is always with me to protect me. I have no need to fear with Him by my side.

Fred (a grown-up boy)

I climbed the backside of the rock with ease as waves lapped and splashed my feet. Behind me, the boat tossed gently, a place of refuge and our vehicle of fun in the summer of 1999.

Confident of my ability to jump into the water from the other side of the massive cliffs, I swaggered my way to the edge, looked down, and was overcome with fear.

One by one, friends and family members jumped into the deep waters of Holston Lake. One guy I didn't even know made me a deal: If he backflipped off the cliffs, I could jump straight in.

He backflipped. I didn't move.

When Fear Wins

That day at Holston Lake was over thirteen years ago, and I could still kick myself for not jumping. I don't like having "I couldn't master that" on my bucket list. But as I looked down at the water that day, my fears took over. They told me the water was shallower than it appeared, or that I might jump too short and hit the jagged rocks.

Fear won the battle for my heart, and I missed out on the amazing feeling of strength and accomplishment that comes with overcoming. It may seem like a small thing to feel frustrated about this many years later, but it taught me something valuable: I want my sons to march headfirst into their life callings without being afraid of what might happen if they fall.

Overcoming Fear

Not long ago, on the Fourth of July, I was watching from the boat as my two little boys stood on a similar rock at Claytor Lake. As a passel of cousins swam below chanting support, my heart flipped and flopped, wondering if I should make them get down. That old familiar fear crept in and told me they were too little to jump from so high. They weren't strong enough swimmers, the water (at thirty feet deep) was too shallow, and they could get hurt.

But something happened this time that changed my perspective. My seven-year-old nephew walked to the edge of the rock, looked down, looked at his mama, and then jumped. He fell into the water, arms stretched wide and eyes full of the excitement of the moment, and yelled . . .

"OVERCOME MY FEARS!"

And then I knew . . .

My boys, at seven and five, are growing longer and stronger each day. And I'm finally beginning to see how God can turn *those boys* who leave me worn out, into *those boys* who will one day change the world. Instead of letting my fears hold them back, I have to let them have the freedom to overcome their own fears. Cultivating a posture of strength in a man is important for five simple reasons:

1. When they're tempted to do what's wrong, they can remember what it felt like to overcome, and draw from that reservoir of strength to choose what's right.

2. The world needs more men who aren't afraid to take a stand, no matter the cost.

3. Their future wives will appreciate a man who isn't afraid to make bold, fearless decisions for the benefit of his family.

4. Their future children will reap the benefits of a father who worships the Lord without fear of what others might think.

5. The kingdom of God will be furthered as men follow hard after their God-given dreams.

Strength in a man, the right kind, is of the utmost importance.

Fist-Pumping Fun

My son's little blond head burst through the water, spraying everyone around him with drops of freedom from fear. Scrawny seven-year-old arms fist-pumped the sky as he yelled, "Yeah! I did it!"

He thinks it was all fun and games, but I know something different. Mama just gave him the opportunity to build his strength. And now, when he encounters the tough, wild, and fearsome the world has to offer, he'll have a full tank of overcomer waiting to flow out of his little manly heart.

He'll know he can conquer what the world throws his way . . . because he already has.

Who knows? Maybe I'll jump with him next time.

PRAYERS FOR OVERCOMING FEAR

May _____ know there is no fear in love, but perfect love casts out fear (1 John 4:18).

May _____ fear You, Lord. For those who fear You have no lack (Psalm 34:9)!

May _____, who fears You, praise You (Psalm 22:23)!

May _____ know that You are his light and salvation— that You are the stronghold of his life; then whom shall he fear (Psalm 27:1)?

May _____ fear not, stand firm, and see Your salvation, which You will work for him today (Exodus 14:13).

May _____ not be afraid or dismayed; may he be strong and courageous (Joshua 10:25).

May _____ be not afraid of those who come against him, nor be afraid of their words, though briers and thorns are with him and he sits on scorpions (Ezekiel 2:6).

May _____ not fear those who kill the body, and after that have nothing more that they can do (Luke 12:4).

May _____ not be afraid of those who come against him, for You declare You are with him to deliver him (Jeremiah 1:8).

May _____ be strong and courageous and not fear or be in dread, for it is You, Lord, our God, who goes with him. You will not leave him or forsake him (Deuteronomy 31:6).

For Reflection or Discussion

1. Have you ever had a challenge that caused you to tuck tail and run? Describe it here.

2. Have you ever felt a bit weak in the knees as you watched your son try something hard or dangerous? Share that experience and how you handled it.

3. Why do you think it's important for men to develop strength?

4. Think back to the experience recalled for question #2. Was your gut reaction to be overprotective of your son or let him have the adventure? Are there areas where you can allow him to spread his wings more?

5. Ask your husband (or another man in your life) what he thinks about letting boys overcome their fears and be adventurous. What are some things you learned from him that can be applied to your parenting?

Integrity

One thing I hate is being called a hypocrite and realizing that they are right in their accusation.

Jamie (a grown-up boy)

Daniel was a young man committed to obeying God. Scripture tells us that he was stolen from his family and country, made to live and serve a people not his own. We know from Daniel 1:1–7 that he had been taken to Babylon because he was considered a youth "without blemish, of good appearance and skillful in all wisdom, endowed with knowledge, understanding learning, and competent to stand in the king's palace. . . ." In other words, Daniel had had some fine raising. At the time of his capture he was already a good, smart boy (not to mention handsome).

The king's desire was for Daniel and his friends to teach him the language of the Chaldeans. I don't know about you, but if I were Daniel's mama I would be so proud! Here's a young man

72

who is not only smart, but so smart he can actually teach others! Don't we moms all want our boys to excel in school? Of course we do! We hope they will get a good education, and that one day all the money and time we've spent on that education will pay off in a successful job. Now, I'm not saying Daniel's mama was happy he had been taken from his home. Rather, I'm suggesting Daniel was a young man a mama could easily be proud to call her own. It sounds like he excelled at everything.

Soon after Daniel arrived in Babylon, though, he faced a decision. The king wanted the boys he had stolen fattened up a bit—both in weight and in knowledge. Daniel and his friends were to be schooled for three years and given daily portions of the king's food and wine. Unspoken, but apparent in these verses, is that the king's food and wine must have broken some of the dietary laws set forth by God. Our smart, handsome, wise, knowledgeable, competent young man had to decide: honor God or honor the king?

Daniel chose God.

And God honored Daniel and used him to draw those around him to Himself.

Which is more important? That Daniel was handsome and well-educated, or that when faced with a choice to sin, he chose obedience?

If you're anything like me, you dream of your son becoming a mighty man of God—a man of integrity, a man of principle, a man who loves Jesus. You dare to hope that when the day of temptation comes, he will stand strong and fight for Truth.

That's the greatest desire of your heart. But I'm guessing you have no idea how to make it happen.

Me neither.

But I do know this: The best parenting in the world cannot make this dream come true. The only way our boys will become like Daniel is for their hearts to be changed. Remember,

Scripture tells us it is God alone who turns hearts of stone to hearts of flesh.

So I'm praying the Lord will give each of my boys a heart like Daniel. A warrior heart set apart for God. A heart of integrity.

PRAYERS FOR INTEGRITY

May _____ walk before You as King David walked, with integrity of heart and uprightness, doing according to all that You have commanded him and keeping Your statutes and rules (1 Kings 9:4).

Till he dies, may _____ never put away his integrity (Job 27:5).

May _____ ponder the way that is blameless and walk with integrity of heart within Your house (Psalm 101:2).

May _____ show himself in all respects to be a model of good works, and in his teaching show integrity and dignity (Titus 2:7).

Like Joseph, may _____ hear Your words, Lord, and obey (Matthew 1:24–25).

Like Daniel, may _____ resolve not to defile himself (Daniel 1:8).

Like Paul, may _____ learn to be content in any situation (Philippians 4:11).

Like Timothy, may _____ be an example to believers in speech, in conduct, in love, in faith, and in purity (1 Timothy 4:12).

Like David with Goliath, may _____ stand up for You, the living God (1 Samuel 17).

Like Abraham, may _____ obey You in faith (Genesis 12:4).

FOR REFLECTION OR DISCUSSION

1. In today's world, the pressure to raise a son who is smart, handsome, funny, and athletic can be intense. How can you make sure your goals and dreams for your son are in alignment with what God says is important for him?

2. What is your response to this statement from Ken Ham, founder of Answers in Genesis? "I would rather my children be ditch diggers and love Jesus, than PhDs and go to hell."

3. In your parenting thus far, have you focused more on your son's accomplishments and life experiences or on teaching him a godly worldview?

4. What temptations or challenges has your son faced so far? How has he handled them? How can you help him handle future challenges in a way that honors God?

5. Does your son have friends who challenge him to be more like Christ? If not, pray God would send friends to provide a positive influence for him.

Wisdom

I didn't have a solid base in the Bible, so I did my own thing. . . .

Lance (a grown-up boy)

In their book *Instructing a Child's Heart*, Tedd and Margy Tripp have this to say about foolishness:

> The Bible's definition of foolishness is concise. *"The fool says in his heart, 'There is no God'"* (Psalm 14:1). If there is no God, I am autonomous—a law unto myself. There is no consideration in life more profound than, *"What will please me?"* Children don't say those words, but such foolish thoughts are the underlying justifications for hundreds of impulses every day. It is expressed in all the acts of disobedience, selfishness, willful temper, and compulsive self-love.[1]

1. Tedd and Margy Tripp, *Instructing a Child's Heart* (Wapwallopen, PA: Shepherd Press, 2008), 112.

As my boys have gotten older, I've spent a lot of time talking to them about the kind of men they want to be when they grow up. I was blessed to be surrounded by good men as a young girl. Men who loved their families hard, served others faithfully, and stood for something greater than themselves. Men who sacrificed so their families could have the best, and taught their children to work hard and protect what they believed in.

I want to continue the tradition of raising good men. But I also know that good isn't enough. I want to raise *wise*, good men. Men who seek the Lord and put Him first in their lives. Men who aren't afraid to stand up for what's right, no matter the cost.

All of life is a choice. And those choices have the power to affect us and everyone we love. So when I talk to my sons about the kind of men they want to be, I tell them there are only two types to choose from: wise or foolish.

The foolish man says in his heart there is no God and acts like a law unto himself. He only cares about what's best for himself, looks out for number one, and serves his own needs first all the days of his life. I like to lean pretty heavy on making this sound like the bad option, and truly, it is. But the good news is, there's another, better way. . . .

The wise man fears and obeys God and has security in the blessings of a loving God and all the power of heaven on his side. With God's help, our sons can submit their lives and hearts to Him and choose to follow the path of wisdom.

Proverbs 8:35 says, "Whoever finds me [wisdom] finds life." I want my boys to love wisdom. I want wisdom to resonate deep within their souls so that it's easy for them to find it and walk in it. And, of course, I want them to live passionate, good lives. The Bible says that finding wisdom IS finding life. Loving wisdom, longing for it, seeking it in every choice they make will provide them the opportunity to live a better, fuller life. Maybe not as the world sees it, but certainly in the eyes of God.

When our boys fight (and let's just throw it out there, shall we? All children fight)—whether it be over toys, who gets to do something first, or just the everyday annoyances that come with living out life in the same house—my husband and I always ask them these questions:

"Who are you choosing to love the most right now? Who are you caring most for in this moment?"

They know the answer: They're caring most for themselves, acting as if they're the only ones in the world whose wants and desires matter, as if they don't have to answer to anyone but themselves. In fact, they're behaving like the foolish man who says in his heart there is no God, no outside authority to answer to.

Proverbs 14:16 tells us, "One who is wise is cautious and turns away from evil, but a fool is reckless and careless." It's true, Mom, we can hold out the truth of the Word of God and allow it to teach our sons! How cool is that? We can begin defining what it is to be a good, honorable, WISE man to our boys from an early age. And if your son is older, you can start now. Show him what the Bible has to say about the wise man and the foolish man, and watch the truths begin to shape his choices one by one.

PRAYERS FOR WISDOM

May _____ be like Solomon and ask You, God, for an understanding mind and the ability to discern between good and evil (1 Kings 3:9).

May _____ find wisdom and therefore find life (Proverbs 8:35).

May _____ be like the wise man who fears You, Lord (Proverbs 14:16).

May _____ get wisdom and insight (Proverbs 4:7).

May _____ listen to the way of wisdom and be led in the paths of uprightness (Proverbs 4:11).

May _____ discern and follow wisdom that is first pure, then peaceable, gentle, open to reason, full of mercy and good fruits, impartial, and sincere (James 3:17).

May _____ say to wisdom, "You are my sister," and call insight his intimate friend (Proverbs 7:4).

Lord, may _____ be filled with the knowledge of Your will in all spiritual wisdom and understanding (Colossians 1:9).

May _____ look carefully in how he walks, not as unwise but as wise (Ephesians 5:15).

May _____ hear Your words, God, and do them, like the wise man who built his house upon the rock (Matthew 7:24).

FOR REFLECTION OR DISCUSSION

1. List behaviors in children you consider foolish, then explain why you consider them to be foolish.

2. Read Psalm 14:1, and then re-answer question #1, defining and listing foolish behavior as the Bible defines it.

3. Why do you think it's important to define our lives (and the words we use) by the Bible's standards?

4. Sometimes our children make foolish decisions. Other times they make poor decisions simply because they don't know better. Describe the difference, and how your correction of each might differ.

5. To help your boy recognize foolish behavior, brainstorm other questions you could add to the ones presented in this chapter ("Who are you choosing to love the most right now? Who are you caring most for in this moment?").

Pride

One's pride will bring him low, but he who is lowly in spirit
will obtain honor.

Proverbs 29:23

Boys are just prone to pride, aren't they? Whether it's hanging
on the basketball rim after a slam dunk, wanting to drive the
fastest car or truck, or joyfully sinking their brother's battle-
ship, pride seems to be deeply ingrained in the hearts of boys.

And it's not all bad.

I actually like the idea of my boys taking pride in what they
do. When they set their minds to something, I want them to
finish well, do the best they can, and encourage those around
them to do the same. I want them to win plenty of games, score
plenty of goals, work hard for plenty of As, and earn plenty
of promotions.

But I also want them to lose some, miss some, and fail some.

Failed Goals

When I was a child, my father was constantly asking what my goals for my life were. Many a night was spent on our couch in the living room talking about stepping-stones, or how to make sure I could achieve my goals. I had my life mapped out before I was sixteen, and I accomplished everything on my list by the time I was twenty-seven. It was a short, somewhat immature list with things like "Graduate," "Get married," and "Have kids" on it. But with God's help I checked them off one by one.

Still, one experience sticks out in my memory when I didn't meet a goal, and the lesson it provided was much more important than the other times I did.

In the spring of 1998, I was a college senior and facing the class I had dreaded: Anatomy and Physiology. I had put the class off as long as I possibly could. I needed it to graduate, but oh, how I longed to skip it. Often touted as the most difficult class at the school, I knew it was going to require maximum concentration and study time.

On the day of our first exam, though, I sat down at my desk completely confident. I had devoted as much time and resources as I possibly could to learning the material, and I felt ready to ace whatever my professor put in front of me.

When grade day finally came, I was horrified to see a large red B across the top of my paper. It was all I could do not to run out of the classroom in tears.

Now, some may wonder why in the world I was so upset over a B? B is good, right? Well, yes and no.

A B meant I passed the exam, which was great. But B also meant that after giving that exam everything I had, I wasn't capable of an A. I felt like the words "she doesn't have what it takes" were stamped across my forehead. That test proved that I had personal, intellectual limits, and I felt like a failure.

Later, as I shared my woes with my dad, he told me a story that changed my life. As an executive at the textile plant where he worked, Dad had the opportunity to be a part of many hirings and, unfortunately, many firings. When describing what he looked for in a new hire, he told me, "I would rather hire a B student who gave that B everything he had and proved his desire to work hard, than hire an A student whose accomplishments came easily and didn't teach him the value of hard work." A good word.

I don't really care anything about raising men who excel at everything. My goal isn't to raise professional baseball players, or even the next president of the United States. My prayer is for my sons to work hard, take pride in what they do, and know the value of not always finishing first. I want them to fail in some things so their pride in their own abilities will be realistic and they'll know their own personal limitations. Sometimes, the greater lesson is in our failures . . . and our limitations are often what lead us to the cross for help.

PRAYERS FOR PRIDE

May _____ not have a haughty spirit, for pride goes before destruction, and a haughty spirit before a fall (Proverbs 16:18).

May _____ be lowly in spirit and obtain honor, for one's pride will bring him low, but he who is lowly in spirit will obtain honor (Proverbs 29:23).

Lord, make _____ turn from doing wrong and keep him from pride (Job 33:17). Lord, please break _____ 's proud spirit (Leviticus 26:19).

May _____ take advice and gain wisdom, for with insolence comes nothing but strife (Proverbs 13:10).

May _____ not be a "scoffer," the name of the arrogant, haughty man who acts with arrogant pride (Proverbs 21:24).

Lord, give us the pleasure of taking great pride in _____ and being filled with comfort (2 Corinthians 7:4).

Let _____ test his own work, and then his reason to boast will be in himself alone and not in his neighbor (Galatians 6:4).

Let not the foot of arrogance come upon _____ , nor the hand of the wicked drive him away (Psalm 36:11).

Let _____ talk no more so very proudly and let not arrogance come from his mouth; for You, Lord, are a God of knowledge, and by You actions are weighed (1 Samuel 2:3).

FOR REFLECTION OR DISCUSSION

1. Did you ever give something your very best shot and still come up short? How did it feel?

2. What do you think about the idea of wanting our children to fail sometimes? Do you agree it is valuable?

3. Learning about our own personal limitations can be humbling and a difficult pill to swallow, but it's still valuable information. List some of your son's weaknesses and then brainstorm ways you can encourage him in them.

4. Are you okay with your son not excelling at everything? Be honest. If the answer is no, spend some time trying to figure out why.

5. What are your dreams for your son? How do they measure up with what God's Word says is truly valuable in a man's life?

Honor

It's standing when a lady enters the room and offering her your chair. It's being a servant leader. It's defending the weak. It's being a man of your word.

Caid (a grown-up boy)

When I talk to my boys about being honorable, it's usually because I want them to represent our family well. Last summer, as my husband and I prepared to drop them off at a local Vacation Bible School, we challenged them to live up to the McGlothlin family name. I reminded them that even a child makes himself known by his acts, by whether his conduct is pure and upright (Proverbs 20:11), and asked them if they wanted to be known for their obedience or for their disobedience. We talked through the implications of their choices, and asked God to help their choices be wise.

It didn't work.

In fact, that might've been their worst night at VBS. Throughout the week as I picked them up and dropped them off, people smiled at me and said, "Those boys of yours sure are energetic!" Which, as all moms of boys know, is code for, "Those boys of yours sure are driving us crazy!"

But you know what? It's okay. At five and seven, they're only just learning the honor in a name, and mistakes pave the way for serious growth. My hope is that as their father and I hold the bar high in this area, they'll rise to the occasion.

The Power of Story

Have you ever sat down with your son and told him your family story? A this-is-who-we-are story gives a boy something to live up to and can help him measure his behavior, goals, and priorities in light of your family's values. For example, in our family, ministering to others is a priority. I do it through my writing, or by cooking a meal for a family in need, serving on the board of directors for my local pregnancy center, telling others about the need for Bible translation in remote parts of the world, and loving and respecting my husband.

My husband ministers to others by watching their homes when they're away, cleaning our house when I'm writing a book, playing football with the boys when I'm not feeling well, mowing the pregnancy center's lawn once a month during the summer, and obeying his boss at work. I also like to tell our sons about honorable things their grandparents or other family members have done—again, to give them something worthy to live up to.

We're working hard to create a vision for our sons of the importance of doing the right thing because it honors God and, well, just because it's the right thing to do. We want to teach them the value of doing the right thing just because it's the right thing, not because they'll get a reward for it, or recognition of some kind, but because we want them to take their reputations seriously and work hard to be known for their honorable names. We've lost some of the "honor of a name" as a society, but I think if we tell our stories to our children, we can work to get it back.

PRAYERS FOR HONOR

Lord, may _____ know that both riches and honor come from You, and that You rule over all (1 Chronicles 29:12).

May _____ fear You and receive honor (Psalm 15:4).

May You, Lord, bestow favor and honor upon _____ . For no good thing do You withhold from those who walk uprightly (Psalm 84:11).

Lord, be with _____ in trouble; rescue him and honor him (Psalm 91:15).

May _____ honor You with his wealth and with the firstfruits of all his produce (Proverbs 3:9).

May _____ be wise and inherit honor (Proverbs 3:35).

May _____ honor everyone and love the brotherhood. May he fear You and honor his leaders (1 Peter 2:17).

May _____ honor his father and mother, for this is the first commandment with a promise (Ephesians 6:2).

May _____ honor the face of an old man (Leviticus 19:32).

May _____ do good, and receive glory, honor, and peace (Romans 2:10).

For Reflection or Discussion

1. What is your family story? Write it down or share it with others.

2. Is your family story an honorable one? Even if it's not, you can still tell it in a way that gives God the glory. Write down how Jesus has redeemed your story and begin trying to think of how to share it, emphasizing the redemptive aspects instead of the failures.

3. In your home or even in your son's bedroom, consider displaying Proverbs 20:11: "Even a child makes himself known by his acts, by whether his conduct is pure and upright." Visit the *Praying for Boys* resource page at www .prayingforboys.com/resources to get a free download for yours!

4. Are you holding the honor-bar high in your family? If not, what are some changes you can make today to raise it?

5. Make a list of all the things your family is doing right.

Purity

I knew it was wrong, yet when that opportunity arose I did not know how to say NO to the temptation.

Jim (a grown-up boy)

Let's cut to the chase, shall we?

Many of us made mistakes with our purity. We either danced too close to the line or blazed right past it without a care in the world. Now, as we prepare to teach and train our boys to save sex for marriage, we're completely lost.

Should we tell them about our failures? Can we expect them to wait when we might not have? Should we just hand them birth control and tell them to be safe?

Many mothers (and fathers) choose to give their sons condoms as a means of protection. As a mom, I understand this completely. I would give my own life to protect my children from being hurt, and I would give most everything else to ensure that they hurt no one. But, as a Christian, I know this truth: "In this world you will have tribulation . . ." (John 16:33). We hope that by telling them to be careful we'll protect them from getting someone pregnant or from putting them in a position where they have to make a choice. But I would submit that doing this communicates a negative message to our sons.

I don't believe we should hold out a "lesser than" standard for our boys. The Bible clearly states that sex is to be lovingly expressed within the boundaries of marriage. End of story. And if we believe the Bible is the Word of God, we need to let *it* be the authority on this delicate issue.

The following are thoughts to consider when talking to your boy about sex.

1. *Your son needs to know you believe in his ability to control himself.*

All of his life he's hopefully heard from you, "I believe you can do this! I believe in you!" Every child needs to know that his parents see something bigger in him—they see potential. He looks to you, whether you like it or not, as an expert, an authority. Parents are supposed to have all the answers, right? If you communicate or even hint that you don't believe your son can control himself, you're risking your relationship with him. *Hey, if Mom doesn't think I'm capable of waiting until marriage, maybe I really can't.* Believe me, that's the last place you want him to be.

Keeping sex for marriage can be done. But you know what? An even better message to send your son—from the time he's a little boy until he's in heaven with his Maker—is that he cannot do it by himself. However, God can do it in him, and He wants to help your son be faithful to His will.

Don't deprive your son of the opportunity to dive to the foot of the cross in desperate need of sovereign intervention. He needs the intensity of the battle. He needs to prove to himself he can overcome. More important, he'll miss the sweetness of victory as Christ meets his every need and becomes the TRUE Lover of his soul.

2. Men were made to protect women. Period.

One of the most important things a man can do is protect a woman . . . from himself. We absolutely must teach our sons to be protectors. It can start with superheroes, move to childhood friends, and find its completion in their lifelong mates. However they get it, I firmly believe men need to see themselves as designed by God to protect, and my hope and prayer is that they'll embrace this call enough to deny themselves pleasure if it means protecting the women they love.

True love denies itself for what's in the best interest of the other.

3. Hold out a vision for the blessings of the pure life.

Purity isn't just about sex. Purity is about keeping our eyes and hearts from anything evil, anything that has the power to overcome our will or turn our hearts away from the only true God.

Purity is about loving God so much that we hate our sin, hate being tempted to sin. Purity is doing just about anything to stay in right fellowship with God.

There can be no substitute for hands that are clean and hearts that are pure before God (Psalm 24:4). It's the better life than one filled with strife, personal angst, and unrest. Peace comes from a pure life, and even has the power to make us healthier. People who go against what they know to be true often experience extreme cognitive dissonance—an unrest of the soul.

But we can't have a vision for the importance of a pure life if we don't love God passionately. So . . . do you love God passionately? Are you seeking Him with all your heart, mind, soul, and strength? Are you choosing the right thing over the easy thing? Your son is watching you. Let him see your love for God bubble over in worship and affect the things you do and say. Then pray for him to fall in love with God too.

PRAYERS FOR PURITY

May _____ have love that issues from a pure heart and a good conscience and a sincere faith (1 Timothy 1:5).

May _____ hope in You, God, and thus purify himself (1 John 3:3).

May _____ have religion that is pure and undefiled before You, our Father: to visit orphans and widows in their affliction, and to keep himself unstained from the world (James 1:27).

May _____ think on whatever is true, whatever is honorable, whatever is just, whatever is pure, whatever is lovely, whatever is commendable; if there is any excellence, if there is anything worthy of praise, may he think about these things (Philippians 4:8).

May _____ be like the pure in heart, for they shall see You, our God (Matthew 5:8).

May there be no violence in _____ 's hands, and may his prayer be pure (Job 16:17).

May _____ be pure, because even a child makes himself known by his acts, by whether his conduct is pure and upright (Proverbs 20:11).

May _____ 's love abound more and more in knowledge and depth of insight, so that he may be able to discern what is best and be pure and blameless until the day he is united with You, Christ (Philippians 1:9–10).

How can _____ keep his way pure? By guarding it according to Your Word (Psalm 119:9).

May _____ be blameless and innocent—Your child, without blemish in the midst of a crooked and twisted generation (Philippians 2:15).

FOR REFLECTION OR DISCUSSION

1. Sometimes parents find it hard to talk to their children about sex because of their own impure pasts. If this describes you, take a minute to ask God to heal what He died to save. It's so much easier to talk about the hard things with our children when we're doing it from a place of health.

2. Do you truly believe teens today can save sex for marriage? Do you feel your answer is based on the world around you or the truth of God's Word?

3. What are the implications of the fact that we're not able to keep pure lives without God's help?

4. In your home and family, are the men allowed to protect the women?

5. Where are you in your walk with Christ? Do you see yourself as someone who is passionately in love with Jesus? What type of relationship would others say you have with Christ?

9

A Servant's Heart

Get them involved in church and sports and scouts and other
activities that encourage serving, especially so they see men
doing it.

Jason (a grown-up boy)

My husband has a servant's heart. It's his gift. During the
first trimester of both of my pregnancies, when I was so
sick I couldn't keep up with the house, he did it all for me. He
never asked what I needed. He never complained or whined. He
just did what needed to be done. I often joke with people and
say he had no idea what to do with *me*, so he just took care of
everything else!

A servant's heart is a great trait for a man to have; I hope it
passes on to my sons! As a mom, I want nothing but the best
for my boys, so every day my husband and I make decisions
that are designed with their best in mind. We hope to see them

make wise decisions so they'll have the best life possible. It's a common desire for moms, and a pure one, but sometimes we take it too far. Consider this passage from Matthew:

> Then the mother of the sons of Zebedee came up to [Jesus] with her sons, and kneeling before him she asked him for something. And he said to her, "What do you want?" She said to him, "Say that these two sons of mine are to sit, one at your right hand and one at your left, in your kingdom."
>
> Matthew 20:20–21

True Greatness

In the few chapters before Matthew 20, we find Jesus teaching the disciples about the true meaning of greatness. The jury's out about whether they really knew who Jesus was at that point, but they did know there was something special about Him. So special, in fact, that they had given up their lives to follow Him. It was only natural for them to ask Him questions, and in true Jesus form, He told them stories illustrating the answers to their questions and challenged them to look at life differently.

And then in Matthew 20:21, the mother of the sons of Zebedee asked Jesus for a specific favor—for her sons to be the favored ones.

Commentaries seem to indicate that this mother was one of the women who attended Jesus during His earthly ministry. It's possible that she may have thought her service to Him so valuable He couldn't and wouldn't deny her whatever she asked. In her, I find a similar heart for my sons.

Every day I ask Jesus to find them, to save them, and to set their feet upon solid ground. I want them to live their lives as close to Him as possible, following hard after His commands and seeking His presence. I think that was this woman's heart too. She was a simple mom who wanted the best for her boys. But she really didn't know what she was asking for. Jesus told her as much in the next verse when He said, "You do not know what you are asking. Are you able to drink the cup that I am to drink?" (Matthew 20:22).

Our hearts tell us we need to be the greatest, that our boys need to be the greatest. But Jesus says the greatest shall be the least.

> You know that the rulers of the Gentiles lord it over them, and their great ones exercise authority over them. It shall not be so among you. But whoever would be great among you must be your servant.
>
> Matthew 20:25–26

One practical way we illustrate this in our home is by actually making the first the last. I doubt there's a mom alive who hasn't had to deal with a case of the "me firsts." So when one of my boys begs to be first, he's automatically last.

We're also trying to help our boys serve others by making the effort ourselves. When a police officer was shot and killed a few years ago on the campus of Virginia Tech (my alma mater), we baked cookies and made cards for each batch that read "Thank you for protecting me," and snuck around after dark delivering them to all of the police officers we could think of who live near our house. The boys thought they were superheroes sleuthing around the neighborhood, and the way I see it, they were—superheroes serving true heroes who give up so much to keep us safe.

We don't *have* to serve others, but Jesus did. And He said if we want to be first, we'll need to be last. My prayer is that my boys will inherit a lifestyle of serving and not shun hard work that brings glory to God, because a life in service to others is truly the most rewarding.

PRAYERS FOR A SERVANT'S HEART

May _____ be Your servant, Lord Jesus Christ (James 1:1).

May _____ follow You; and where You are, may _____ be also. For Your Word says, if anyone serves Christ, the Father will honor him (John 12:26).

May _____ be like Moses, faithful in all Your house as a servant (Hebrews 3:5).

As Your servant, may _____ not be quarrelsome but kind to everyone, able to teach, patiently enduring evil, correcting his opponents with gentleness (2 Timothy 2:24–25).

May _____ not use his freedom to satisfy his sinful nature. Instead, may he use his freedom to serve others in love (Galatians 5:13).

May _____ use his spiritual gifts to serve others, as a good steward of Your varied grace (1 Peter 4:10).

May _____ serve wholeheartedly, as if he were serving You, Lord, not men (Ephesians 6:7).

Let _____ be grateful for receiving a kingdom that cannot be shaken, and let him offer to You acceptable worship, with reverence and awe (Hebrews 12:28).

May _____ be a servant, for the greatest among us shall be servants (Matthew 23:11).

May _____ fear You, his God, and serve You only (Deuteronomy 6:13).

For Reflection or Discussion

1. Have you ever felt like the mother of the sons of Zebedee? Ever wanted to ask God to lift up your boys and favor them over others?

2. Sometimes it's tempting to think God owes us a specific answer to prayer in return for all we've done for Him. If you have struggled with this in the past, how so?

3. In your own life, how are you serving others?

4. Now brainstorm ways you can serve that would be great training opportunities for your boy.

5. What are some fun ways you can teach your boy about the "first shall be last" concept?

Fruit of the Spirit: Love

Anyone who does not love does not know God, because God is love.

1 John 4:8

In this chapter we take our first step into two of my favorite verses to pray for my sons. I pray Galatians 5:22–23 most every day, if not in their entirety, at least in part. If I could choose only one passage to pray for my boys for the rest of their lives, it would be my second choice (behind Ezekiel 36:26), because having hearts full of love, joy, peace, patience, kindness, goodness, faithfulness, gentleness, and self-control just about sums up everything I want for them.

So let's start with love.

The Bible says, "God *is* love" (1 John 4:8). For you mathematicians, using the word *is* is the same as using the word *equals*. In other words, God and love are one and the same. God = Love.

There is no real love apart from God, and God is behind all genuine acts of love.

Can I make a bold statement? If our sons don't have God, they can't truly love. I know that seems pretty harsh, but I believe it's true. Men tend to equate love with the physical, women the emotional. And certainly the fullness of God's nature is found in both aspects of love. But without God, love is often reduced to superficial, self-serving, pleasure-seeking feelings. Even with Him it can be hard to get rid of all our selfish reasons for loving.

Just recently, when a friend went through a difficult season in his marriage, my sons learned what the word *divorce* means. It broke my heart to hear my oldest son say, "I didn't know you could get unmarried." The boys had such a difficult time trying to understand why two people who had once loved each other would ever want to stop being married.

The only answer I could give them was that sometimes people choose a selfish kind of love (it was a simple answer, I know, and I'm not trying to indicate that divorces are ever simple or aren't sometimes necessary) instead of choosing to love even when they don't feel like it.

Real love, like God's love for us, never gives up. May our sons always know and offer that kind of love.

PRAYERS FOR LOVE

May _____ not love the world or the things in the world (1 John 2:15).

God, may all your sons love one another, for Your Word says love is from God, and whoever loves has been born of God and knows God (1 John 4:7).

May all your sons love one another earnestly from a pure heart (1 Peter 1:22).

May all your sons, when they become husbands, love their wives as their own bodies. For he who loves his wife loves himself (Ephesians 5:28).

May You, Lord, make _____ increase and abound in love (1 Thessalonians 3:12).

May _____ know that this is love: that we walk according to Your commandments (2 John 1:6).

May _____ not love in word or talk but in deed and in truth (1 John 3:18).

May mercy, peace, and love be multiplied to _____ (Jude 1:2).

May _____ love You, Lord, his God, with all his heart and with all his soul and with all his might (Deuteronomy 6:5).

May _____ know that this is love, not that we have loved You, God, but that You loved us and sent Your Son to be the propitiation for our sins (1 John 4:10).

For Reflection or Discussion

1. How do you define love?

2. Have you ever considered that true love (the best, most perfect kind) can't exist apart from an empowering relationship with God?

3. Do you have that kind of relationship with God? If not, what do you need to do to get it?

4. What are some ways having God's love can help us to love others better?

5. Are you showing the "never give up" kind of love to your sons? What are some practical steps you can take to begin doing that today?

Fruit of the Spirit: Joy

Not sure I had an understanding of joy as a boy.

David (a grown-up boy)

As I write these words, I'm struggling with a deep desire to be grumpy and complain. Ever had a day like that? Most days I handle my husband's crazy shift-work schedule pretty well. But today? Well, today I feel like complaining. So how do I find joy and strength from the Lord? How do you? The world has the definition of joy all wrong. But what is it really? And if my strength comes from the joy of the Lord (Psalm 28:7), then what does the joy of the Lord really look like?

Several years ago I made a connection between Psalm 28:7 and Psalm 16:11. One says the joy of the Lord is our strength, the other says it's in the Lord's presence that we find fullness of joy. It makes sense, then, that if I want to find strength for the day-to-day, if I want a life filled with joy and not just fading happiness, I'll need to find my way into the very presence of God . . . because that's where the fullness of joy lives.

But where in the world do I find the presence of God? And how do I lead my boys there so they're not seeking after fleeting happiness but pursuing deep and abiding joy?

Draw near to God, and he will draw near to you.

James 4:8

Yes, the simplest answer is often the best one. Need to hear God speak to you? Need to know He's working, moving in your life? Need to feel the joy of the Lord, the unspeakable joy of knowing that Christ took the full punishment for your sin? Get close to Him.

Over the years I've found a few ways to invite my household into God's presence.

1. The Peace Chair

I have to admit I adapted this concept from writer Ann Voskamp.[1] She calls it a peace retreat, but whatever you call it, I believe it's a nice twist on a time-out. Instead of removing your child to the time-out space to be left to his own thoughts and devices, you're calling him away for some time alone with Jesus to refresh and refocus his mind on Christ.

At our house, the peace chair lives in the dining room. Because our boys are still young, I find it best to be able to see and hear them as they sit to pray and reflect so that I can redirect them if I need to. Older boys could probably handle the time spent in their rooms, away from everyone else, with clear directions and expectations from Mom. We provide for them a basket of

1. Ann Voskamp, "How to Make and Take a Peace Retreat," A Holy Experience, April 1, 2011, www.aholyexperience.com/2011/04/how-to-make-take-a-peace-retreat-right-where-you-are/.

age-appropriate books on prayer and knowing God to browse and read while they're sitting there, as well as some pleasant lighting to help their little souls relax into beauty. I also have a verse I pray for them every day framed and hanging right above their heads to remind them of why they're sitting there.

It may seem like a superficial change to the time-out theory of correcting behavior, but I believe it goes much deeper. Training our children from a young age to go to the only One who has the power to change their hearts can have lasting life implications. Heaven knows they'll always need to run to Jesus to help them overcome.

2. Pray out loud

I've met a lot of people in my time who are deathly afraid of praying out loud. Can I respectfully ask you to get over it, friends? I don't mean to sound uncaring or disrespectful, but hearing a person pour out her heart in prayer is like having a window into the heart. What you believe about God often comes out in prayer, and it can be an amazing way to help your boys understand the character of God and model how to draw near to Him.

3. Let your son see you worship

This is really an extension of praying out loud. Even if you're not an expressive worshiper, let your son see you take joy in praising God. And worshiping God goes beyond singing—any act of obedience to God communicates your devotion to Him and speaks volumes to your son about where you find your joy and peace.

4. Share your brokenness

Psalm 34:18 says, "The LORD is near to the brokenhearted and saves the crushed in spirit." Let your boy see how God ministers to you when you're broken. Tell your son how God is taking care of you. Help him believe in the God who takes care of the needs of His children.

5. Let him have quiet time with you . . .

. . . when he's old enough. Until then, let your son find you often at the Word of God, the wellspring of life, studying it and seeking to know God more through His love letter to His people.

PRAYERS FOR JOY

Lord, may Your joy be _____ 's strength (Nehemiah 8:10).

May _____ be filled with love, joy, peace, patience, kindness, goodness, faithfulness, gentleness, and self-control (Galatians 5:22).

May _____ go out in joy and be led forth in peace (Isaiah 55:12).

May You, the God of hope, fill _____ with all joy and peace as he trusts in You, so that he may overflow with hope by the power of Your Holy Spirit (Romans 15:13).

May _____ go to Your altar—to You, God, his joy and his delight (Psalm 43:4).

May _____ count it all joy when he meets trials of various kinds, as the testing of his faith produces steadfastness. May he let steadfastness have its full effect, so that he may be perfect and complete, lacking in nothing (James 1:2–4).

May _____ know that while weeping may tarry for the night, joy comes with the morning (Psalm 30:5).

May _____ be imitators of us and of You, Lord (1 Thessalonians 1:6).

May _____ be like David, and dance before You with joy (2 Samuel 6:14).

May _____ know that Your kingdom is not a matter of eating and drinking but of righteousness and peace and joy in Your Holy Spirit (Romans 14:17).

FOR REFLECTION OR DISCUSSION

1. Reflect a moment on your life. Where do you find the most joy? Is it in the right place? Why or why not?

2. Do you struggle to pray out loud or be expressive (even just a little!) in your worship? Ask the Lord to show you why.

3. Think of one way the Lord has met your needs recently that you could share with your boy.

4. Do you find yourself pursuing temporal happiness more than the everlasting joy that comes from knowing Jesus? How does that affect your son?

Fruit of the Spirit: Peace

Now may the Lord of peace himself give you peace at all times in every way. The Lord be with you all.

2 Thessalonians 3:16

As a child I was terrified of the dark. Not just your average run-of-the-mill child's fears either—I mean I was TERRI-FIED of the dark. I slept with a nightlight until I was way into my late teens and continued to struggle even into my early adult years. I have never felt safe sleeping in a house alone, not at my parents' house, not in my school apartments, and not even after I was married.

I can't tell you how many sleepless nights I've suffered because of this gripping, paralyzing fear of being vulnerable to attack. The only thing I knew to do to face my fear was to read the Bible for hours before trying to go to sleep at night. But honestly, it never helped.

About a year after my husband and I were married, I took a job three hours away. We wanted to move closer to our hometown and believed he would get a transfer sooner or later, so I packed up my stuff and moved without him, spending my weeks there working and my weekends back with him.

One night after eating dinner, taking my dog for a walk, and trying unsuccessfully to get him calm enough to let me sleep, something happened that changed my life forever. Someone tried to break into the house where I was living, and although my dog's vicious lunging at the door and ferocious bark probably scared the guy off, I was left in a puddle of fear, crouching in a corner of my bedroom with my hands over my head.

In that moment, I felt the fiery darts of the Enemy hurling at me and assaulting my fears. I knew I had a choice to make: let my fears completely take over my life, or overcome my fears. Because of God's grace, I decided to take a step of faith and overcome, and I did it with prayer.

Do you remember that old children's prayer we all learned when we were little? It's been reproduced so many times, in so many ways, that it's pretty much ingrained in the hearts and minds of children everywhere:

> Now I lay me down to sleep
> I pray the Lord my soul to keep.
> If I should die before I wake
> I pray the Lord my soul to take.

(Seriously, I just typed that without even having to Google it.) It reminds me of my battle with fear and the victory God allowed me as I called out to Him. I call it *Now I PRAY Me Down to Sleep*, and, really, that's exactly what I do. When I find myself alone in a home, even my own, needing to fall asleep and fighting the familiar old fears, I start praying. I ask the Lord to give me the peace that only He can bring. Then I ask Him to fill my mind with friends, family, co-workers, or even random people who might need my prayers. I literally pray myself to sleep, and it works every single time.

Why? Because I'm taking my mind off of my cares and worries and asking God to fill it with the things He cares about. Peace that surpasses understanding fills my heart and soul, and I drift off to dreamland.

God is the giver of peace. Fear is a lack of peace. As Christians, we (and our sons) will battle to grab peace in a world that doesn't have enough of it. Prayer connects us to the heart of God—taking our minds off of us and placing our attention on Him. Prayer is the BEST way to find peace and overcome the fears of the world. Plus, this concept is so easy to teach to our sons.

Training can start at a young age. But no matter how old your son is, when he expresses fear, immediately pray over him and let him know that fear is not from God (2 Timothy 1:7). Then, when you're comforting your son, ask him who he'd like to pray for. When you're done, pray for someone else, and then someone else. Train him to focus his mind away from himself and his own fear and onto the needs of others. It took me more than thirty years to realize this truth—that it is indeed more blessed (and more peaceful) to give than to receive (Acts 20:35), and that by thinking and praying for others first, I lose sight of my own troubles and find my heart and mind truly at peace. Your son doesn't have to wait.

PRAYERS FOR PEACE

Let _____ turn away from evil and do good; let him seek peace and pursue it (1 Peter 3:11).

Lord of peace, may You give _____ peace at all times in every way (2 Thessalonians 3:16).

Leave Your peace with _____, for You do not give as the world gives. Let not _____'s heart be troubled, neither let him be afraid (John 14:27).

May _____ be joyful and grow to maturity. May he encourage others and live in harmony and peace. Then You, the God of love and peace, will be with him (2 Corinthians 13:11).

May _____ sow a harvest of righteousness by making peace (James 3:18).

Let the peace of Christ rule in _____'s heart, to which indeed he was called in one body, and be thankful (Colossians 3:15).

May mercy, peace, and love be multiplied to _____ (Jude 1:2).

May Your peace, which surpasses all understanding, guard _____'s heart and mind in Christ Jesus (Philippians 4:7).

May _____ be justified by faith and have peace with You, our Lord Jesus Christ (Romans 5:1).

God of peace, may You sanctify _____ completely, and may his whole spirit and soul and body be kept blameless at the coming of our Lord Jesus Christ (1 Thessalonians 5:23).

FOR REFLECTION OR DISCUSSION

1. What is your greatest fear?

2. Have you overcome it? If so, how?

3. Have you ever been in a situation that caused your fears to come to life? How did you respond?

4. Has your boy struggled with fear? In what ways?

5. Make a list of people in your life who need prayer, and keep it by your bedside (or your son's) so you'll never have a shortage of prayer material.

Fruit of the Spirit: Patience

I didn't have too much patience as a boy. I tended to let my emotions get out of control when stressed.

Tom (a grown-up boy)

Because of television and the Internet, our boys will grow up with no shortage of glamorous people to look up to. They'll be tempted to look at their lives and think that to really matter in this world, they'll have to do something big. But that's not the truth. I'm convinced God cares less about how much we accomplish in life—the "great things" we do in His name—than He does about how we respond to the daily things He allows us to experience. Some of the most accomplished people in the kingdom of Christ are those whose names you and I will never know this side of heaven; greatness is only measured by how well we respond to Christ in the little things.

Great Patience

I sat across the table from a younger friend of mine recently and listened to her share her heart and vision for all she wanted to accomplish in Jesus' name. She was sixteen at the time and had decided that living an everyday, mundane life wasn't for her. No, she wanted a big life spent for the Lord. My friend was looking at what is often mistaken for the glamorous Christian life, and missing the blessings of the small.

Paul Miller, in his book *A Praying Life,* described a woman who struggled with the world's definition of greatness:

> Underneath her obedient life is a sense of helplessness. It has become part of her very nature . . . almost like breathing. Why? Because she is weak. She can feel her restless heart, her tendency to compare herself with others. She is shocked at how jealousy can well up in her. She notices how easily the world gets its hooks in her. In short, she distrusts herself. When she looks at other people, she sees the same struggles. The world, the flesh, and the devil are too much for her. The result? Her heart cries out to God in prayer. She needs Jesus.[1]

I don't want my boys to aspire to greatness by the world's standards, or to feel that they must do something big in order to count for the kingdom of God. But if there's something children (and adults, for that matter) have trouble with, it's waiting. I have trouble with it myself. My mom used to call me "Bee in the Bonnet Boo" because . . .

1. My nickname is Boo. (You are NOT allowed to use that against me!)

2. When I decide I want something, what I really mean is that I want it YESTERDAY.

1. Paul E. Miller, *A Praying Life* (Colorado Springs: NavPress, 2009), 56.

We all struggle with patience. It's much harder to wait and be faithful to God in the small things than it is to get the glory all at once. But I believe Romans 5:4 when it says that perseverance produces character, and character—who we really are in our hearts—is what God is after the most.

My little boys often hear me say I need to see them be faithful in the small things before I can give them the responsibility of the big things. They don't like it, but it's the general way of the world and a good lesson to learn early on.

Then, *if* God ever gives our boys the big dreams of their hearts, they'll have the substance to be ready for it.

PRAYERS FOR PATIENCE

May _____ be an example of suffering and patience (James 5:10).

Lord, may _____ be strengthened with all power, according to Your glorious might, for all endurance and patience with joy (Colossians 1:11).

May _____ prove himself by his purity, understanding, patience, and kindness, by Your Holy Spirit within him and by Your sincere love (2 Corinthians 6:6).

May _____ preach the Word and be ready in season and out of season; may he reprove, rebuke, and exhort with complete patience and teaching (2 Timothy 4:2).

May _____ not presume on the riches of Your kindness and forbearance and patience, knowing that Your kindness, God, is meant to lead him to repentance (Romans 2:4).

May _____ put on then—as one of Your chosen ones, holy and beloved—a compassionate heart, kindness, humility, meekness, and patience (Colossians 3:12).

May _____ be patient, for the patient in spirit is better than the proud in spirit (Ecclesiastes 7:8).

May _____ have good sense, making him slow to anger, for it is his glory to overlook an offense (Proverbs 19:11).

May _____ make every effort to add to his faith goodness; and to goodness, knowledge; and to knowledge, self-control; and to self-control, perseverance; and to perseverance, godliness; and to godliness, brotherly kindness; and to brotherly kindness, love (2 Peter 1:5–7).

May _____ be sober-minded, dignified, self-controlled, and sound in faith, in love, and in steadfastness (Titus 2:2).

FOR REFLECTION OR DISCUSSION

1. We've all probably been guilty at some point of desiring the big things in life. What are some of your big dreams?

2. What big dreams do you have for your son? How might it be possible for those to get in the way of the "small" things that God wants to work in his life first?

3. What's your nickname? (Just kidding!)

4. Do you struggle with waiting on the Lord? How might this affect your son?

5. How can you affirm the little victories in your son's life, letting him know that overcoming in small ways, each and every day, is important too?

Fruit of the Spirit: Kindness

Put on then, as God's chosen ones, holy and beloved, compassionate hearts, kindness, humility, meekness, and patience.

Colossians 3:12

His grubby little hands carry a load of dusty baby books downstairs that we don't read anymore, while his precious growing-up-more-every-day heart carries a burden I'm not entirely sure he is ready for but have faith that God will use somehow. I have no idea what my son is doing with all of those books when he is supposed to be in quiet time, but when I see the prices on them, I suspect it might have something to do with a project our family has taken on recently. I'm right.

I began blogging for The Seed Company when my heart was struck by the sheer volume of people in our world who don't even have one verse of God's Word in their heart languages. Current statistics tell us that over 340 million people need the Bible translated into their languages. Many of those people don't even have a written language! So as you can imagine, the process can be slow and tedious.

The Seed Company was founded to accelerate this translation process and bring the good news of Jesus Christ to all nations, fulfilling the Great Commission of Matthew 28. One group The Seed Company is working with are the people of the Democratic Republic of the Congo (DRC). Many live in constant fear of attack, rape, pillaging, death, and theft of their children from militant rebels who hide out in the nearby Rwandan hills. The DRC so grabbed my heart when I heard their story that my family has adopted them as our prayer focus, and my MOB Society family of writers offers the proceeds of our first e-book, *From Mom's Failure to God's Grace: Stories of Raising Boys from the MOB Society Writers*, to help with the translation efforts there.

Twice in the last year I've been notified of a brutal attack on these precious people—once with reports of women and children being tortured and killed, the other with Seed Company field translators fearfully hiding under their beds with their small children as the rebels took over the city.

It was after the last notification that I decided to share the news with my sweet little family. I prepared a list of thirty Scripture prayers for the people of the DRC (you can find a free, downloadable copy of it on the *Praying for Boys* resource page), and we committed to praying for them every day for a month. At this writing, I don't have any updated information on how our prayers have affected the people over there. I don't have a specific story to tell you of how God used our prayers to save someone's life or further the gospel. But I do have a story of what it's done in a little five-year-old boy's heart.

He walked downstairs with all of those books, laid them down in front of me, and told me that when he grew up he was going to become a ninja so he could fly over to the DRC and save the children there. Then he informed me that selling these books we don't read anymore and giving the money to the DRC would have to do for now (because he's not a ninja yet).

My heart overflowed with joy, and I was able to overlook the fact that he took some of my favorite baby books and wrote dollar amounts on them with a Sharpie. No, what mattered was my little boy wanted to *do something*. My crazy, wild, 250 percent boy was thinking about someone other than himself, beyond our four walls, willing to give up something he loved in order to bless *someone else*. It was a hallelujah moment.

Kindness. It roots its way into the hearts of our children when we give them something to care about, tell them a story that's greater than they are, and help them see the real, present needs of those around them.

My little guy is terribly sensitive to small things. He has a collection of baby stuffed animals like you wouldn't believe, and I truly think he would bring home every stray animal we could find if they would just stay babies forever. When we lost our third baby to a miscarriage in 2011, he took it harder than my older son because he had prayed and asked God to give us a baby for over a year. In light of those things, I wasn't sure telling him about what's happening in the DRC was wise. He struggles with nightmares sometimes too, and I didn't want to give him any more scary visuals to think of as he's trying to fall asleep.

But we did tell him, and now I couldn't be more glad because of how God is using it to work in his heart (not to mention his future career path as a ninja—wink, wink; it might be cool to have one in the family). I can see a seed of kindness taking root, and it's more rewarding than most anything else.

If you and your family would like to get involved in the Bible translation work of The Seed Company, find out more at www .theseedcompany.org.

PRAYERS FOR KINDNESS

Lord, may You now show _____ love and faithfulness
(2 Samuel 2:6).

May _____ be kind and tenderhearted to others, forgiving, just as Christ forgave him (Ephesians 4:32).

May _____, as Your servant, not be quarrelsome but
kind to everyone, able to teach, patiently enduring evil
(2 Timothy 2:24).

May _____ never repay anyone evil for evil but always
seek to do good to others and to everyone (1 Thessalonians
5:15).

Let _____'s speech always be gracious, seasoned with
salt, so that he may know how he ought to answer each
person (Colossians 4:6).

May _____ love others with brotherly affection and
outdo others in showing honor (Romans 12:10).

Lord, may You bless _____ and keep him. May Your
face shine upon him and be gracious to him; turn Your
face toward him and give him peace (Numbers 6:23–26).

May _____ not neglect to show hospitality to strangers, for thereby some have entertained angels unawares (Hebrews 13:2).

May _____ see how good and pleasant it is when brothers dwell in unity! (Psalm 133:1).

May _____ live in harmony with others; may he be sympathetic, show brotherly love, and be humble (1 Peter 3:8).

FOR REFLECTION OR DISCUSSION

1. Are there any ministries the Lord has put on your heart? If so, how can you involve your boy in them?

2. Have you ever considered that sharing the hard things of life with your son (in an age-appropriate manner) might open his heart to generosity and kindness?

3. If our sons don't know what's happening in the world, how can the Holy Spirit motivate their hearts to serve? Think of some greater need in your community or the world to share with your son, and together purpose to pray for that need for thirty days.

4. List five ways your son has exhibited kindness over the last month. Then go to him and praise him for them.

5. Gather together a group of your son's peers and have a random acts of kindness day. Ideas include serving in your community, reading to children at your local homeless shelter, collecting diapers for your local pregnancy care center, or handing out pre-written blessings to strangers at the mall.

15

Fruit of the Spirit: Goodness

Oh, how abundant is your goodness, which you have stored up for those who fear you and worked for those who take refuge in you.

Psalm 31:19

My seven-year-old son sat down in front of me recently and asked me the question many parents around the world fear: "Mom, is Santa Claus real?"

My husband and I have never played the Santa Claus card hard in our home, but neither have we tried to dissuade our boys from believing in the magic of the whole thing. We've worked to make sure they understand the true meaning of Christmas, but we don't judge our friends who work just as hard to enjoy their kids' delight in the story of the grand old elf.

One thing we have done is talk up the story of St. Nicholas. We even bought the cute *Veggie Tales* movie by the same title and show it every year just to make sure they know who he was and where the legend of Santa Claus started. We knew one day our boys would ask the question, and we felt like the story of St. Nicholas was a perfect way to explain why some families, including ours, pretend he's real.

We don't have a lot of historical facts about the life of St. Nicholas. Legends galore exist to explain his importance, most of them probably not true, or at the least exaggerated to the point of being unrecognizable. What does seem to be consistently told about him is he was born to a wealthy Christian family and his parents died when he was young. Scholars also believe he had a penchant for giving in secret—possibly to save poor girls with no dowry from a life of prostitution, possibly just to keep needy people from starving. In my opinion, the *Veggie Tales* movie does a decent job of presenting basic facts about St. Nicholas in a way that grabs the attention of children and helps them understand the true spirit of giving. That's why it's my favorite Christmas movie.

There's a part in the movie when Nicholas's father explains to him that the reason their family is so generous, so *good*, is because God has been so good to them. In the movie, it takes Nicholas years, and much soul-searching, to understand the kind of love that changes a person so deeply he or she is compelled to share it with others. But he eventually does, and as the legend goes, his love for God compels him to bless others. Something to aspire to, indeed.

So as my son looked at me with questioning eyes, I told him St. Nicholas was a real person, and parents all over the world celebrate the spirit of what he did by pretending to do something similar with their own children. But we mustn't forget why Nicholas gave in the first place—because he had been given much first. Not gold, not silver, not fancy presents, but simply the love of a radically good God.

It's the goodness of God that compels us to be good.

What other response is there, really, to a God who bends down to listen to His people (Psalm 116:2 NLT)? How else should we show our gratitude for the God who took on flesh and suffered for our sins when we deserved every stripe, every insult, every nail?

When we truly understand the depth of God's gift of salvation and where we would be without it, we're motivated to do good works and live a good, moral life. We're motivated to give because God gave to us. We love to love, because of the way He first loved us. And we love to point others to Him because we know He can give them the same gifts He's given us.

PRAYERS FOR GOODNESS

May _____ be glad of heart for all the goodness that You have shown to his people (1 Kings 8:66).

May goodness and mercy follow _____ all the days of his life, and may he dwell in Your house forever (Psalm 23:6).

O Lord, remember not the sins of _____'s youth or his transgressions; according to Your steadfast love, remember _____ for the sake of Your goodness (Psalm 25:7).

May _____ believe that he shall look upon Your goodness in the land of the living (Psalm 27:13).

How abundant is Your goodness, which You have stored up for _____ and worked for those who take refuge in You, in the sight of the children of mankind (Psalm 31:19).

May _____ be satisfied with the goodness of Your house, the holiness of Your temple (Psalm 65:4).

May _____ taste the goodness of Your Word (Hebrews 6:5).

It is not good that _____ should be alone; Lord, make him a helper fit for him (Genesis 2:18).

May _____ do what is right and good in the sight of You, Lord, that it may go well with him (Deuteronomy 6:18).

May _____ go and celebrate because of all the good things You have given to him (Deuteronomy 26:11).

For Reflection or Discussion

1. Have you ever told your son, "Just be good"? Has your understanding of the word *good* changed since reading this chapter?

2. Teaching our sons to be good for the sake of being good is much different from being good as a response to the goodness of God. How will you explain the goodness of God to your children?

3. Name five ways the Lord has been good to you in the last month.

4. What are some things you can say or do with your boy to help him see how God is good to him personally? To your entire family?

5. What are some activities you and your family can do together that give back to your community?

16

Fruit of the Spirit: Faithfulness

His master said to him, "Well done, good and faithful servant. You have been faithful over a little; I will set you over much."

Matthew 25:23

I recently polled our MOB Society community on the definition of a faithful man. This is what they had to say:

A faithful man is _____ (fill in the blank).

- Hot!
- Honest
- Bold!
- Priceless
- A man of God
- A man of his word
- A treasure

- A girl's dream
- Hard to find
- Such a blessing!
- Confident in the Lord
- Not to be taken for granted
- Priceless and hard to find
- A gift to his family
- A glory to God!
- A jewel!

I agree! A faithful man is all of these things and more. We all want our boys to grow up to be faithful husbands, faithful givers, faithful providers, faithful to God, and on and on. But a state of being faithful *to* something they can't see or touch with their fingers is difficult to teach, especially as boys are growing up and forming their own opinions about God and the world around them. I think it might be a bit easier to teach them to be faithful *with* what God's given them—their time, talents, gifts, and loved ones—first. Here's a little story that helps me better understand how to do this.

In Matthew 25:14–30, Jesus tells what has become known as the parable of the talents. In this story, the master entrusts his servants with money to keep and care for during his absence. You might remember that two of the servants do well, doubling their money in the time the master is away. But the third servant performs poorly and is only able to give back to the master what was given to him.

I researched this passage quite a bit, and one of the things I found in *Matthew Henry's Complete Commentary of the Whole Bible* is that this passage can be used to show we constantly live in a state of work and business. A good work ethic and strong business knowledge serve us well in life. Learning the art of business is a choice—an action we take to better ourselves and provide for our loved ones. Surprisingly, so is faithfulness.

In the parable, the master *trusted* his servants with gifts. And Jesus, our Master, has entrusted His servants with the good gifts that come in our lives when we trust in Him (James 1:17). He desires for us to be faithful with them, growing them for use in His service. We are the ones Jesus has entrusted with His earthly ministry. In His strength and indwelled by His Holy Spirit, we are to represent His will and be faithful with what He's given us. Faithfulness, then, by definition, is a good work, an action, a choice, to spend wisely the good gifts we're given from God.

It's important as we help groom our sons and begin recognizing the gifts God has given them, that we help them understand why they have those gifts. God desires for all of our gifts to bring Him glory. That doesn't mean we have to use our gifts in a church, or in public ministry, but it does mean we should use them in a way that would make Him smile in approval. Here are a few ways to teach your boy to be faithful with what God's given him:

- Is he musical? Let him perform at a nursing home, bringing joy to those who need it desperately.
- Is he athletic? Lead him in reaching out to those who aren't. Sports bring an amazing opportunity to invest in the lives of others, and to make those who feel small, feel big.
- Is he super smart? Suggest he offer his time to help a classmate understand the subject better.
- Is he good at making money? Lead him in tithing, and every once in a while suggest he donate whatever stash he has to a worthy organization or need in your church.

I want to prepare our boys to be faithful now with what God's given them so they'll be prepared to do it themselves later. It may even translate into being more faithful in all areas of their lives because they're learning early that what they have really isn't theirs. Wouldn't it be nice if more pro athletes, celebrities, and musicians understood their talents were given to them not to puff them up but to bring joy to others?

The one servant from the parable in Matthew who failed to grow and develop what he'd been given was chastised for missing an opportunity and failing to understand the ways of the master. God doesn't give us gifts so we can hoard them or use them only for our benefit. He doesn't care how big our talents are, only that we use them for Him. Teach your son to be faithful with what God's given him, and pray a root of faithfulness will grow in his heart.

PRAYERS FOR FAITHFULNESS

May _____ fear You, Lord, and serve You in sincerity and in faithfulness (Joshua 24:14).

May _____ fear You and serve You faithfully with all his heart, considering what great things You have done for him (1 Samuel 12:24).

Lord, all Your paths are steadfast love and faithfulness for _____ as he keeps Your covenant and Your testimonies (Psalm 25:10).

May Your steadfast love be before _____'s eyes, as he walks in Your faithfulness (Psalm 26:3).

May _____ trust in You, Lord, and do good; may he dwell in the land and befriend faithfulness (Psalm 37:3).

May You never remove from _____ Your steadfast love or be false to Your faithfulness (Psalm 89:33).

Lord, cover _____ with Your pinions, and under Your wings may he find refuge; Your faithfulness is a shield and buckler to _____ (Psalm 91:4).

Let not steadfast love and faithfulness forsake _____; may he bind them around his neck; write them on the tablet of his heart (Proverbs 3:3).

May _____ call this to mind and therefore have hope: Because of Your great love he is not consumed, for Your compassions never fail. They are new every morning; great is Your faithfulness. May _____ say to himself, "The LORD is my portion; therefore I will hope in him" (Lamentations 3:21–24).

No temptation has overtaken _____ that is not common to man. You are faithful, and You will not let him be tempted beyond his ability, but with the temptation You will also provide the way of escape, that _____ may be able to endure it (1 Corinthians 10:13).

FOR REFLECTION OR DISCUSSION

1. How would you finish this statement? A faithful man is
   _____ (fill in the blank).

2. How are you showing faithfulness with what God's given
   you?

3. If everything we have really belongs to God, how should
   we treat our possessions? Hold them tightly, or with open
   hands?

4. Are there areas of your life in which you need to give up
   control and let God use you and your gifts more faithfully?

5. Make a list of some of your son's gifts. Sit down with him
   and make a plan for one way he can be faithful with them
   in the next week.

17

Fruit of the Spirit: Gentleness

Sometimes we are taught that it's weak to be gentle, but we need to learn it in order to function in the real world, especially when we have kids of our own!

Dale (a grown-up boy)

'Ve been on the bottom of too many wrestling piles to believe that aggression in men isn't commonplace. It may not manifest itself in the same way for all of them, but it's there nonetheless. For the physical boys, it shows up in their need to be on the *top* of the wrestling pile (or their inability to quit wrestling when Mom and Dad are completely worn out). For the intellectuals, it shows up in their need to score the highest on the exam or be at the top of the class (or feel like a failure when they make anything other than an A).

Personally, I don't think there's anything wrong with a little aggression. I don't want to break my sons of their aggressive streak, and I'm learning not to be afraid of it. But I do want to teach them how and when to use it. One of the best ways I can think of to do this is to train them in gentleness (no easy feat, I understand).

One of my sons (who shall remain nameless) has some good friends in his class at church. They're a ragtag bunch of fearless boys who all love the Lord the best they know how, but they also feed off of each other: When one is wound up, the others get there quickly. More than once I've seen the word *exhaustion* written all over their teacher at the end of Sunday school. Having a class full of boys is rough for any teacher, any time, but when all of the boys in class are what I like to call "those" boys (you know, the ones who are 250 percent boy?), an hour's worth of Sunday school can leave a girl completely worn out.

To help our sons get their brains and hearts in the right place before entering church, my husband and I pray for them before we even get out of the car. As soon as we pull into our parking spot (or maybe even on the way if we're running late), we pause, grab hands if we can, and ask the Lord to ready our hearts for worship. We specifically pray and ask God to help them see opportunities to serve their friends, and help them to know the difference between playtime and listening time. The last thing out of our mouths as they walk into their classrooms is, "There's a time to play and a time to listen."

It isn't foolproof, but I've found that pausing to get our minds on why we're there can be so helpful. Let's face it, Sunday mornings can be some of the *most* stressful times in a Christian family's life. There have been way more arguments in our family than I care to admit as we run around like crazy people trying to get out the door. Refocusing gives us a chance to reconnect, say we're sorry, and humble ourselves before the Lord.

It also has the potential to completely turn the tide of our emotions and help redirect all that aggression into something the boys can use for the Lord and His kingdom. They need to know what we expect of them in each situation, and why we do what we do, so they can learn to control themselves and understand how their behavior affects everyone around them.

As a bonus, here's a list of some of our other favorite phrases to use as reminders with our rough and tumble boys on the road to gentleness:

- God made men to protect women and care for them.
- God made you a big brother! Your job is to protect your little brother, not hurt him.
- If you can't listen, you have to feel (this one has been passed down through several generations of my family, and is true in so many aspects of life).
- God wants you to use your strength to protect, not to hurt.
- Superheroes don't look for fights, but they will fight to protect others.
- It's okay to want to be the best, but the best people in life are the ones who serve others.
- A gentle answer turns away wrath (Proverbs 15:1).

PRAYERS FOR GENTLENESS

May _____ know that a gentle tongue is a tree of life, but perverseness in it breaks the spirit (Proverbs 15:4).

Lord, may _____ take Your yoke upon him and learn from You, for You are gentle and lowly in heart; then _____ will find rest for his soul (Matthew 11:29).

May _____ be completely humble and gentle, patient and bearing with others in love (Ephesians 4:2).

May _____ be gentle, like a nursing mother taking care of her own children (1 Thessalonians 2:7).

May _____ not be a drunkard, not violent but gentle, not quarrelsome, not a lover of money (1 Timothy 3:3).

May _____ pursue righteousness, godliness, faith, love, steadfastness, and gentleness (1 Timothy 6:11).

O God, may _____ correct his opponents with gentleness, that You may perhaps grant him repentance leading to a knowledge of the truth (2 Timothy 2:25).

May _____ speak evil of no one, avoid quarreling, be gentle, and show perfect courtesy toward all people (Titus 3:2).

May _____ have wisdom from above that is first pure, then peaceable, gentle, open to reason, full of mercy and good fruits, and impartial and sincere (James 3:17).

May _____ honor You, Christ the Lord, as holy, always being prepared to make a defense to anyone who asks him for a reason for the hope that is in him, yet do it with gentleness and respect (1 Peter 3:15).

FOR REFLECTION OR DISCUSSION

1. How do you feel about aggression in boys? Is it something you're comfortable with or afraid of?

2. In what way is your son aggressive?

3. What are some practical ways you can help your son redirect his aggression?

4. Think of three or four places or situations where your boy needs to practice more gentleness. Talk to him about how he can be more gentle in each situation.

5. What phrases are helpful (or could be) in your family to encourage gentleness?

Fruit of the Spirit: Self-Control

A man without self-control is like a city broken into and left without walls.

Proverbs 25:28

Not long ago, my husband and I lost our beloved English bulldog, Deacon. It was devastating, as he was really our first son, our furry son, if you will. Deacon was ten years old, and we knew he was nearing the end of his life-span, but that didn't make his loss any easier.

Friends and family surrounded us because they knew how important this dog was to us. My husband's brother helped him dig the large hole we required to bury a big, stocky dog; a colleague of my husband's bought us a coin jar to help us save for our next furry friend; and a dear friend offered to let us have one of his son's purebred Labrador retrievers . . . absolutely free.

And so Toby the yellow Lab found his way to our home.

Right away we knew Toby was going to be a big boy. I've always wanted a large-breed dog, but I also knew that if he was going to integrate well into our home, he would have to have some serious training. The last thing I wanted to happen was to have to give away a large dog we loved just because we couldn't control him, so we enrolled him in a local obedience class.

Some friends of ours agreed to watch our boys for us while we took Toby to class each week, and the boys had a blast hanging out with them. They played football, climbed trees, tackled each other, messed up their good jeans, and peed on a bush in front of a nice restaurant in front of the mall.

Yes, I did just say my boys peed on a bush in front of our entire city.

In their defense, the restaurant wasn't open yet and they really had to go. The other thing you should know is my husband and I do occasionally allow our sons to pee on trees, but never in public! The bottom line is, they would NEVER have done that if we had been there, and they knew when they got home that they were in trouble.

My husband and I pondered what to do with these crazy boys that would cause them to pause the next time they were tempted to do such a thing. Really, at seven and five, they're most of the way beyond the "I have to go RIGHT NOW" stage. And even though there are still times of urgency, there was no reason for them to think pulling their pants down in front of God and everybody was okay. We knew this was a lesson in self-control.

Learning to regulate their behaviors is one of the hardest things for boys to do. I can't tell you how many times I've whispered (okay, maybe not a whisper) to one of my sons, "That behavior is not acceptable!" I feel like a broken record most of the time, but I have faith that over time it will start to sink in.

I can honestly say we are beginning to see some light at the end of the behavior tunnel (aside from the Great Pee Incident, as it is now known). In one summer's time, my seven-year-old matured what seems like seven years. He's become easier to handle, better behaved (most days), and is beginning to genuinely care about someone other than himself. Much of the stress we feel because of our boys' behavior will be outgrown in time. I can see that now, when I couldn't before. I thought they would always be little misfits in the behavior department, and while they may always be harder to handle than other boys their age, they are beginning to show some signs of improvement.

Self-control isn't learned overnight. Many adults struggle with self-control. I know I do! It's part of our sanctification in Christ and part of learning to die to ourselves daily. Big thoughts for such little people.

I'm happy to report that our boys haven't peed in public since that day. We ended up making them write "I will not pee in public" twenty times and had them apologize to our friends who were keeping them. And as for Toby the dog, turns out self-control is hard for him too. There's a pretty female dog who lives next door. . . .

PRAYERS FOR SELF-CONTROL

May _____ know that he is Your temple and that Your Spirit dwells in him (1 Corinthians 3:16).

May _____ not let sin reign in his mortal body, making him obey its passions (Romans 6:12).

May _____ not present his members to sin as instruments for unrighteousness, but present himself to You as one who has been brought from death to life, and his members to You as instruments for righteousness (Romans 6:13).

May _____ present his body as a living sacrifice, holy and acceptable to You, God, which is his spiritual worship. May he not be conformed to this world, but transformed by the renewal of his mind, that by testing he may discern what is Your will, what is good and acceptable and perfect (Romans 12:1–2).

May _____ discipline his body and keep it under control, lest after preaching to others he himself should be disqualified (1 Corinthians 9:27).

Whether _____ eats or drinks, or whatever he does, may he do it all to Your glory (1 Corinthians 10:31).

Let not _____'s heart envy sinners, but continue in the fear of You, Lord, all the day (Proverbs 23:17).

Remove far from _____ falsehood and lying; give him neither poverty nor riches; feed him with the food that is needful for him (Proverbs 30:8).

Let the words of _____'s mouth and the meditation of his heart be acceptable in Your sight, O Lord, his Rock and his Redeemer (Psalm 19:14).

May _____ have a tranquil heart that gives life to the flesh (Proverbs 14:30).

May _____ be wise in doing right and stay innocent of any wrong (Romans 16:19).

For Reflection or Discussion

1. Recall some funny stories (well, maybe they're funny now . . .) of ways your boy has exhibited a lack of self-control.

2. How did you turn those times into lessons? If you didn't, take a minute to think about how you could have.

3. We all (and I mean ALL) struggle with self-control in some way. What are your weaknesses?

4. Are you seeing any (any at all) light at the end of the tunnel for your boy? When you do, pause to really breathe these victories in and take them to heart. Allow them to encourage you in your journey.

5. Have you ever made your boy apologize to someone for something he did? Why do you think it's valuable?

Anger

Boys can get really angry when the men in their lives don't respect them. They need to have that sense of male approval.

Todd (a grown-up boy)

So much of the Christian life is a choice. Every day (multiple times a day) we have the opportunity to choose God or ourselves, choose to say "yes" to God or "yes" to ourselves, choose to do what's right in the eyes of God or what's right in our own eyes.

Anger is a perfect example. You can just feel it coming, can't you? Anger is an almost total body experience. Muscles get tight. Temples throb. Jaws clench, and explosion feels imminent, wooing us into believing we have no choice but to react.

But it's not true.

We almost always have a choice when it comes to anger (or reacting to any other emotion, for that matter). We can choose

149

to embrace it and sin, or we can put it aside and instead choose kindness, self-control, compassion, and love.

My oldest son started taking fiddle lessons when he was just four. For the last four years we've invested an enormous amount of time, energy, and money into his gift. About a year ago my youngest started taking lessons too. As a mama, there's not a whole lot that brings me greater joy than watching them work together to create beautiful music.

That's why, when I heard that our local pregnancy center was hosting their annual fund-raising banquet with a Beethoven theme, I asked if they might like to have two little fiddlers be a part of the program, for which six hundred people or so were expected.

(Some of you are puzzled right now, trying to figure out how fiddling and Beethoven go together. Let me assure you, a violin and a fiddle are the same instrument. The only difference is how you play it. Our boys are actually taking violin lessons; we just like to call it a "fiddle" here in the South.)

After the banquet organizers said "yes" to my boys' performance, we started four months of preparation that kicked . . . My. Tail. It left me asking myself, *Why in the WORLD did I offer to do this?!?*

Ode to Joy?

The last week before the banquet, in particular, was grueling. We practiced our arrangement of *Ode to Joy* about ten times a day, putting aside normal schooling that week for the sake of working hard to be a blessing to a worthy ministry. Mama (that's me) also released a new e-book that same week called *How to Control Your Emotions, So They Don't Control You.* Yes I did. And it was a bit on the crazy side. Yes it was.

I don't think I've ever experienced so much stress. My boys waltzed through it without batting an eyelash. They didn't seem nervous at all, but heaven knows I was nervous enough for everyone.

Truth be known, I was wiped. And when I get wiped, I struggle to control my emotions. Little things bother me that wouldn't otherwise, and it's a major effort to keep from snapping at everyone around me. Ironically, that last week before their performance was a perfect test for controlling my emotions. There were a few times I failed just a little, others where I almost failed, and one time I failed royally. But overall, I was able to embrace the simple truth of Proverbs 9:6: "Leave your simple ways, and live, and walk in the way of insight."

You see, I've allowed my emotions to control me too many times. I can tell when I'm nearing the danger zone, or as I like to call it, the downward spiral of emotions. For a long time, though, I didn't really care. If I wanted to get angry, I got angry, and if anyone tried to tell me I didn't have a right to get angry, it made me even angrier.

I thought I had a right to feel any way I wanted to, whether my feelings were accurate or not, simply because they were my feelings.

Wrong.

I've learned these last few years that this way of thinking is not only unbiblical but also highly destructive. What I can see with my eyes and feel with my heart isn't always the truth. In fact, if I'm feeling out of control, I've probably embraced the lie that what I want is more important than glorifying God in every situation of life.

God gave us our emotions as a barometer—something to alert us that there might be something off in our surroundings or in our hearts—but He didn't give them to us to rule our lives, or dictate our behavior. He wants to rule our lives. And when we're in Christ, we already possess the power to overcome. We just have to choose it.

Practically Speaking

I have a child who tends toward the dramatic. In reality, he's a lot like me—emotional. When he doesn't get his way, or he feels unfairly treated, he spouts off. Over the years I've learned that what comes out of his mouth (and mine, for that matter) is really a reflection of what's in his heart. When he feels mistreated, it's because his little heart feels unloved. When he gets mad and yells, it's because he wants something he can't have and feels like no one else is more important than he is.

Aren't most of us like that? When someone hurts me, I react out of the need to protect myself, forgetting that God has told me in His Word that He is my protector, my defender, my shield. The truth is what God says in His Word, no matter what my feelings tell me. And as a Christian—one who has given her life to Christ and committed to following Him—I have the power to choose the truth over my emotions.

So does my little guy. The words, "This is a perfect time to control your emotions! Go ask Jesus to help you!" are becoming a part of our daily routine—as much for him as for his mama. With God's help, as we choose the truths found in His Word over what we can see, feel, or hear, we are overcoming. You can too.

PRAYERS FOR ANGER

May all bitterness and wrath and anger and clamor and slander be put away from _____, along with all malice (Ephesians 4:31).

May _____ put them all away: anger, wrath, malice, slander, and obscene talk from his mouth (Colossians 3:8).

May _____ give a soft answer, which turns away wrath, and avoid harsh words, which stir up anger (Proverbs 15:1).

May _____ not be quick in his spirit to become angry, for anger lodges in the bosom of fools (Ecclesiastes 7:9).

May _____ never avenge himself, but leave it to Your wrath, for it is written, "Vengeance is mine, I will repay, says the Lord" (Romans 12:19).

May _____ know that You are our peace (Ephesians 2:14).

May _____ make peace, and so have a harvest of righteousness (James 3:18).

Let the peace of Christ rule in _____'s heart, to which indeed he was called in one body. And be thankful (Colossians 3:15).

May Your peace, God, which surpasses all understanding, guard _____'s heart and mind in Christ Jesus (Philippians 4:7).

May _____ turn away from evil and do good; let him seek peace and pursue it (1 Peter 3:11).

FOR REFLECTION OR DISCUSSION

1. Take a moment to revisit your own struggles with anger. Do you find it more difficult to keep your emotions under control in particular situations, such as when you're stressed?

2. Have you experienced times when you did not care if your emotions were under control?

3. Have you ever considered that your emotions could be wrong, or that they could lead you in the wrong direction, away from the truth of God's Word?

4. What do you think about the statement that as Christians, we have the power to choose truth over our emotions?

5. If it's true that our emotions reveal what we really believe in our hearts (for example, "I'm the most important!" or "No one loves me!"), what do you think your emotions are revealing about you?

20

Forgiveness

I'm learning to man up and take responsibility for my actions.

Troy (a grown-up boy)

We've all heard a little one, caught by his mommy in a deliberately sinful act, say, "Sorrryyyy." But does it really mean anything? Probably not.

Tedd and Margy Tripp in *Instructing a Child's Heart*, advise giving "children big truths they will grow into rather than light explanations they will grow out of."[1] I agree. That's why from the very beginning I've tried to teach my boys the difference between saying "I'm sorry" and "Please forgive me." The simple but profound difference between the two lies in the person's intent. When someone wounds me or generally does something that affects me adversely, it's either done on purpose or it isn't.

One of the most awe-inspiring, wonderful blessings of being in relationship with Jesus, the Christ, is His all-encompassing,

1. Tedd and Margy Tripp, *Instructing a Child's Heart* (Wapwallopen, PA: Shepherd Press, 2008), 45.

life-giving, life-changing grace. The Bible says Jesus took the full punishment, the wrath of God, in our place. His grace and forgiveness are worth more than a lifetime of riches and gold. Nothing compares to being free from the power of sin and resting in the peace of God's grace and forgiveness, but that forgiveness didn't come cheap.

When to Use "I'm Sorry"

In our home, we say we're sorry if the result of our behavior was an accident. When my oldest son knocks my youngest on the floor trying to get to Daddy when he gets home, he can be sorry because it was an accident. When my youngest slams a hard ball into his daddy's face while playing in the front yard, he can be sorry—it was clearly an accident (and yes, that actually happened—knocked my husband right off the pitcher's mound). Some behaviors can be clearly identified as accidental. The appropriate response, then, is to apologize for inconveniencing another person.

Another example of accidental behavior that can be more difficult to distinguish is childish foolishness. This occurs when our children do silly, harmful, but age-appropriate things, clearly lacking the ability to have prevented them. Both kinds of behavior, clearly accidental or childish foolishness, require an apology. It might go something like this: "Little brother, I'm so sorry I knocked you down. I was so excited to see Daddy that I didn't think. Are you okay?" Or, in the case of our little guy, "Daddy, I'm so sorry I hit a home run in your face." Good grief.

When to Ask for Forgiveness

The need for forgiveness occurs when a child (or an adult, for that matter) has deliberately sinned against another. When little Johnny hits his younger brother out of anger because younger brother won't share, he has sinned. When little brother steals little Johnny's toy right from his hands, he has sinned.

(Please notice: I said "steal." It's important to think of our children's behaviors—and our own—in terms of biblical language. Stealing is breaking one of the Ten Commandments and produces a little sinner in need of salvation. "Taking" someone's toy is much less obvious and can confuse a child's ability to see their behavior as described in the Bible. Using biblical lingo helps keep the Bible relevant and helps us to see our sin in its true light.)

It is sin to deliberately choose one's own desire in spite of the way it affects or hurts someone else, and sin requires repentance, forgiveness, and restoration. Maybe it sounds a little like this: "Big brother, will you forgive me for hitting you? I was choosing to care more about that toy than I was your feelings or safety."

Often it's the simplest distinctions that have a profound effect on the way we understand the world. Asking for forgiveness is humbling because we have to admit a wrongdoing and take responsibility for the sin in our hearts. What a beautiful lesson for the men we're raising to learn. Let's help them know how, when, and why to ask for forgiveness, and pray God develops repentant hearts and spirits within them.

PRAYERS FOR FORGIVENESS

May _____ believe in You, Christ, in whom we have redemption, the forgiveness of sins (Colossians 1:14).

May _____ know that with You there is forgiveness (Psalm 130:4).

May _____ have redemption through Your blood, Jesus, and the forgiveness of his trespasses, according to the riches of Your grace (Ephesians 1:7).

May _____ repent and be baptized in Your name, Jesus Christ, for the forgiveness of his sins (Acts 2:38).

May _____ forgive others if he holds something against them (Mark 11:25).

Heavenly Father, may _____ forgive others their trespasses, as You forgive his (Matthew 6:14).

May _____ forgive his brother from his heart (Matthew 18:35).

May _____ be kind to others, tenderhearted, and forgiving others as You in Christ forgave him (Ephesians 4:32).

May _____ know that to You, Lord, our God, belong mercy and forgiveness (Daniel 9:9).

May _____ remember that You are ready to forgive, are gracious and merciful, are slow to anger, and are abounding in steadfast love (Nehemiah 9:17).

FOR REFLECTION OR DISCUSSION

1. Many studies show that withholding forgiveness affects us not only spiritually but also physically. Has forgiveness been a stumbling block in your life?

2. What is your understanding of forgiveness? Have you tried to teach your son the difference between asking for forgiveness and offering an apology?

3. Can you recall a funny example of when it was okay for your son to offer an apology, such as the "I'm so sorry I hit a home run in your face" incident described in this chapter?

4. Have you ever asked your son to forgive you for sinning against him? Why? Why Not?

5. Has there ever been a moment of deep forgiveness between you and your son? Recall what that moment meant to you.

21

Salvation

But Mary treasured up all these things, pondering them in her heart.

Luke 2:19

It's Christmas, and the four of us sit gathered around the table, by candlelight, faces framed in light, hearts open to the Light as our Advent reading reminds us of the Reason for the season. We pray and then eat, and it's relatively quiet—an anomaly in a house full of boys.

The most amazing things can happen over chili beans at Christmas.

My oldest slams his fist on the table out of nowhere, and the light leading Mary to Bethlehem shakes with the force of it. Lately he's been asking harder questions, like why he has to be kind to others when they aren't required to be kind to him. Tonight his question throws my heart for a loop and I nearly choke on my chili beans.

"What is so important about Jesus?"

I wasn't prepared, and his slamming the table sets the jabbers off in his little brother, who leans in and makes trouble and won't stop. My heart is in shock that my eldest doesn't know the answer, when his whole life I've tried to show him Jesus. My breath is taken away for a second, and while I try to communicate a lifetime of understanding in five-year-old lingo, I notice that his eyes and his heart are far from me. He says as much: "Mom, I can't pay attention when my little brother is acting like that."

A great sadness washes over me as I realize I can't address the question because of his brother's childish foolishness.

The last few days with him have threatened to break my resolve. He's pushed me to the limit, this oldest son of mine, and I've been much on my knees praying for the wisdom that will let me reach his heart.

I clean up dinner. We go on with the night, read our children's Advent book before bed, and say our prayers. He prays for his family—that we'll love each other better—and asks God to help him be kind. His little brother prays for his daddy to be safe as he goes to work later, and I pray for wisdom in this thing called motherhood—always for wisdom.

Then Daddy and little brother leave for bedtime snuggles and I, in turn, snuggle up to this little boy who pushes me to my end over and over again. This one who God uses to keep me on my knees and to break my vanity and my self-righteousness. But in this moment God shows He works ALL things together for good (Romans 8:28) by reaching into the heart that I pray for daily—the one I ask Him to change from stone to flesh—and He makes it flesh.

Eye-to-eye and nose-to-nose, my oldest asks again . . .

"Mommy, why is Jesus so important?"

Moments like these are priceless, and I've learned that sharing the gospel with our boys is more than just a one-time event.

They see the gospel in our hearts by the way we live our lives, the choices we make to honor God, and as they hear our prayers.

There's nothing more important to me than the salvation of my children. I'm sure you feel the same way. Let's pray for God to soften their hearts to His Truth, and empower us to live the Truth in front of them every day.

PRAYERS FOR SALVATION

May _____ confess with his mouth, "Jesus is Lord," and believe in his heart that You raised Jesus from the dead, and be saved (Romans 10:9).

May _____ be saved by grace through faith—not of his own doing, but by Your gift (Ephesians 2:8).

May _____ believe in You who saved us and called us to a holy calling, not because of our works but because of Your own purpose and grace, which You gave us in Christ Jesus before the ages began (2 Timothy 1:9).

May _____ fear not, stand firm, and see Your salvation, which You will work for him today (Exodus 14:13).

Lord, may You be _____'s light and his salvation; whom shall he fear? May You be the stronghold of his life; of whom shall he be afraid? (Psalm 27:1).

May _____ take the helmet of salvation, and the sword of Your Spirit, which is Your Word (Ephesians 6:17).

May _____ work out his own salvation with fear and trembling (Philippians 2:12).

May _____ be guarded through faith for a salvation ready to be revealed in the last time (1 Peter 1:5).

Lord, make Your face shine on _____; save him in Your steadfast love (Psalm 31:16).

Lord, save _____ to the uttermost as he draws near to You through Christ (Hebrews 7:25).

For Reflection or Discussion

1. Can you recall a time when you sensed your son's heart was soft to the message of the gospel?

2. Does your son know the Lord? Where is he in his walk with Him? Where would you like him to be?

3. Have you seen specific ways God brought something beautiful from a situation you thought was lost with your son?

4. In what ways do you strive to make the message of the manger come alive in the heart of your son?

5. Have you made it a habit to pray for the salvation of your son? How has this study changed the way you pray for him so far?

Conclusion

Behold, I am doing a new thing; now it springs forth, do you
not perceive it? I will make a way in the wilderness and rivers
in the desert,

Isaiah 43:19

The one thing I want you to know about me is that I'm just
a mom—just like you. There's nothing particularly special
about me or my two sons. My boys aren't super spiritual or even
always well-behaved, and they need Jesus just as much as their
mama and daddy do . . . all the time and in every way.

You see, I didn't ask the Lord to make me a prayer warrior, but
seven years of a painful stripping, letting the facade of control
slip away, brought me to my knees.

Two sons born twenty-three months apart, driving me to the
edge and back every single day, stripping my pride, leaving me
begging God for a miracle.

Struggling to nurse my firstborn.

A wreck that nearly took my grandmother's life and two
others.

The Virginia Tech shootings, where we lost a friend, and my husband (as a first responder) was so deeply affected by what he saw.

Father's older brother dies on my son's first birthday.

Father's younger brother dies ten months later—same genetic lung disease.

Grandfather dies less than one year later.

Favorite aunt dies a few months later, two years to the day after her husband, my father's youngest brother, died.

A miscarriage one year later.

Grandmother fading away in her memories to dementia.

Why do I pray? It's not because I have all the answers; it's because I don't.

Prayer: The desperate cry of a mama whose life has taught her she has so little control.

I cannot hold my children tightly enough to protect them from all harm, cannot force these brothers to love each other well, cannot control their actions, cannot keep them from losing the people they love, cannot ensure that they will turn out to be the men I dream they will be, cannot make them love the Lord.

I cannot change their hearts of stone to hearts of flesh (Ezekiel 36:26).

Prayer is the coming to the end of ourselves, letting go, and placing our hope in the God who *can*. Like Samson's parents, who believed in the Lord "who works wonders" (Judges 13:19), a lifestyle of prayer consists of putting none of my hope in what *I* can do, but all of my hope in what God has already done. It's taking comfort in a God who loved deeply enough to save me and resting in the knowledge that He can do the same for my sons. It's choosing to believe the truth of His Word, praying for its completion in the hearts of my sons, washing it over my tired heart, and keeping my eyes on the One who straightens my path. It is enough for me and enough for my sons.

I wear a posture of prayer as a lifeline of hope—a desperate plea to the God who works wonders, asking the Lord to empower me and my family by His Spirit.

There are several men of the Bible who experienced the Spirit or power of the Lord just when they needed it. Samson was one of them. When he fought the Philistines, "the Spirit of the LORD rushed upon him, and he went down to Ashkelon and struck down thirty men of the town and took their spoil" (Judges 14:19).

David, the man after God's own heart, was another. The Spirit of the Lord came powerfully over him when he was anointed king by Samuel (1 Samuel 16:13), and there were other times when "the covering," as my friend Cliff Graham likes to call it, fell on Samuel and gave him the power and strength to achieve the tasks God laid before him.

This covering, the Spirit of the Lord, is something I have begun praying will fall on my own sons (and myself) when they are called upon to do battle. The way that happens is a little different post-cross of Jesus than it was in the Old Testament times, but God still gives us the power we need to achieve things for His glory. In the Old Testament, He gave His Spirit for specific times and situations. Now, as believers in Jesus, we have the Holy Spirit actually indwelling us. Really, it's a miracle, if you think about it! We have access this very minute to the same power and strength that allowed David to kill Goliath, Samson to kill thirty Philistines in one fell swoop, and Moses to part the Red Sea. It lives within us because we've placed our faith in Jesus' work on the cross and is available to us when we need it. It's what gives us the ability to stop and choose not to let anger overtake us. It gives us the strength to keep loving when we've been hurt and failed, and it gives weary boy-moms the ability to get down on their knees one more time in prayer for their sons, doing battle in the heavenlies for the hearts of their boys at home.

My heart—and I pray yours too—is that our boys will be fiercely dependent on the Holy Spirit of God at work in their lives. As they battle a world that may seem to be against them at every turn, I pray they'll intentionally access the Spirit of God indwelling their hearts to rise above and be victorious. I pray I'll do the same thing.

My desire for this book is for boy-moms in the trenches of motherhood to be encouraged to get in the battle for the hearts of their sons. I hope to see God change the world as mamas humble themselves and pray. But the bonus to all this praying is the effect it will have on our own hearts if we let it. Prayer connects us deeply with the heart of God. It shows our utter dependence upon Him for most everything, and helps us walk more closely aligned with His will for our lives. May you find more of Him and His strength for your life as you pray for your son.

21 Days of Prayer for Sons

This book grew from a short e-book I wrote a few years ago. Back then I had no idea what God would do with it, but the last thing I wanted was for someone to purchase the book and stick it on her virtual shelf and never use it. I truly believed God wanted to use this message to get moms to pray for revival in the hearts of their sons, so I began praying for God to show me a way to encourage people to use the content of the book. Thus was born the 21 Days of Prayer for Sons prayer challenge.

The first challenge attracted just over two hundred participants. I was overjoyed that so many would want to pray for their sons with me! I started a Facebook page to help get the word out and began writing my heart out to engage everyone in a meaningful discussion about prayer. My little blog got more traffic during that time than it ever had before, and I began to be known as "the prayer girl."

After that initial challenge, emails poured in asking me to lead it again, except this time the participants wanted more. Instead of just daily blog posts, they wanted me to help them lead their own online studies and in their own communities. As a result, the second 21 Days of Prayer for Sons, held just a few months later, launched with a new leader's guide and had over two thousand participants from seven different countries! Each prayer challenge has grown since then, and I've been blessed to see God move in so many amazing ways as moms get on their knees for their sons.

The following guide is loosely based on the first one I created and equips you to lead the 21 Days of Prayer for Sons prayer challenge for groups online, in your church, or in your community. In it you will find help for planning your challenge, as well as resources and encouragement for interacting with other participants. The prayer challenge is designed to be completed over the course of about six weeks, with twenty-one days (or more, if you'd like!) especially focused on praying for the things boys need most. Participants meet together virtually or in real life to encourage, challenge, and pray for the other members of the group.

Each person will need a copy of *Praying for Boys*. Feel free to pull quotes from the book or use the chapter-ending questions to aid in your leadership, but it's not necessary. The questions and information in this book are designed to take your group deeper and may be used any way you like.

Again, what follows is specific help for those who want to lead the group in their church or community, or for those who want to lead an online study of the book on Facebook or their blogs. Choose the way you'd like to lead the study, then flip to the section that best applies to you.

Above all, 21 Days of Prayer for Sons is a prayer challenge designed to help moms take their eyes off of their own parenting skills (or lack thereof) and place them on the One who can turn hearts of stone to hearts of flesh (Ezekiel 36:26). So on behalf of all boy-moms everywhere, I want to thank you for leading this study. I truly believe we'll change the world as we pray for our sons. You're doing something of inestimable value and fighting for the future as you get on your knees.

Serving together,
Brooke

Leading a Church or Community Study

Participants who choose to take the challenge as part of a church or community group should plan to meet together once a week for six weeks to pray together and discuss the prayer challenge. Members are encouraged to stay connected with each other via daily emails or by some type of online forum.

The following is a sample schedule, but feel free to change it to meet the needs of your group.

Sample Schedule

Week One: Participants should read the Foreword and "Boys Are a Battle Zone" before the meeting and come prepared to discuss this material.
Homework: Read "What Is Prayer, and Why Should We Do It?"

Week Two: Discuss the contents of "What Is Prayer, and Why Should We Do It?"

Homework: Read "Going It Alone."

Week Three: Discuss the contents of "Going It Alone."
Homework: Begin the 21 Days of Prayer for Sons challenge, praying the prayers for one topic each day, ten times a day (chapters 1–7).

Week Four: Use the questions at the end of chapters 1–7 to help the participants dig into the prayer topics a little deeper (see Facilitating Group Discussions below for more information).
Homework: Pray the prayers for one topic each day, ten times a day (chapters 8–14).

Week Five: Use the questions at the end of chapters 8–14 to help the participants dig into the prayer topics a little deeper (see Facilitating Group Discussions below for more information).
Homework: Pray the prayers for one topic each day, ten times a day (chapters 15–21).

Week Six: Use the questions at the end of chapters 15–21 to help the participants dig into the prayer topics a little deeper (see Facilitating Group Discussions below for more information). Wrap up the study.

Resources

Church or community group studies will want to have the following items available:

- registration table
- registration cards
- name tags and markers
- Bibles, pens, and pencils
- tissues

Leader's Responsibilities

The leader should be someone with at least one son or grandson (any age). She needs to be interested in exploring the role of prayer in raising godly sons and long for more dependency on God in her parenting. Leaders need not be perfect parents to lead (as if any such thing exists) and do not have to be seasoned moms of older boys. A heart that has been prepared by God and is available, vulnerable, and teachable is more important. Leaders must be committed to seeing the prayer challenge through to its end and encouraging group members to keep going even when they're tempted to quit. Leaders should commit to praying daily for the group during the study, and also

- Provide administrative leadership (organizing and keeping momentum alive for the group).
- Meet weekly with their group.
- Promote the study and make enrollment easy.
- Make sure all participants have copies of the book.
- Provide daily encouragement via email or some type of online forum.
- Take prayer requests from the group and lift them up daily.
- Provide a sense of community (responding to comments, questions, etc.).
- Promote fellowship in any way possible among group members.
- Take notice of opportunities for ministry.

Facilitating Group Discussions

The purpose of small-group discussions is to begin applying what is learned during the week to everyday life. Members should be encouraged to share how God is working in their lives or their sons' lives, new things they've learned from reading the Scripture prayers daily, and how God is changing their views of the place of prayer in parenting. While offering help to other moms is encouraged, group discussion is not intended to be a time to assert one parenting philosophy over another. *Praying for Boys* is not so much a book about the hows of parenting as it is the hows and whys of prayer. Encourage moms to take their eyes off of their own parenting skills during this time and place them on God, who can turn hearts of stone to hearts of flesh (Ezekiel 36:26).

When meeting, arrange room furniture in a circle so all members are facing each other. Don't allow any one member to feel isolated, and make plenty of tissues available and easy to access.

Start your meeting on time!

At the beginning of the first session, ask members to prepare their prayer requests for each week ahead of time on index cards (you may want to provide the index cards for them), and tell them there will be time for group prayer at the end of the meeting. This prevents any one member from taking up all of the time with her prayer request and helps all members feel equally important. Remember to leave plenty of time at the end of the session (approximately two minutes suggested per group member) for prayer. Have members switch cards for the prayer time and pray over someone else's needs. Instruct each member to keep the card all week in a confidential place, and commit to praying over it at least twice before the next meeting.

Spend about an hour discussing the week's prayer topics, encouraging everyone to participate, but not pushing those who wish to remain quiet. Use the questions at the end of each of the main chapters to aid in your discussion when necessary. If it becomes clear a member is distressed during the discussion time, stop and pray immediately.

Make members feel as comfortable as possible. Remember, you are not required to teach your members how to be good mothers. Rather, your job is to encourage them to share based on their experience of the material from *Praying for Boys*. If at any time you feel unqualified to deal with a situation in your group, don't hesitate to call in the help of your pastor or other responsible authority.

If, during the course of your study, you become aware that a group member is unsaved, commit to speaking with her about it privately and NOT during group time. Listen to the Holy Spirit and invite the member to lunch, or offer to have her over to your house one day that week. NEVER make a member feel the group is waiting for her to make a decision about salvation.

Define clear boundaries with your group members. This is vital to the group dynamic! Don't allow any one member to take over the group or talk through the entire meeting. Gently redirect her back to the material. If more action is required, offer to talk to the member after class. If a member becomes hostile or abusive in any way, gently remind her to be kind and compassionate toward the group members. If the behavior persists, ask her to leave.

End your meeting on time!

A Note on Confidentiality

A member's ability to feel safe in sharing her heart and prayer needs is absolutely crucial to the group dynamic. Please announce to your members during the first meeting that all personal information should be kept strictly confidential.

A Note on Parenting Styles

There are as many different parenting styles as there are models of cars, but the Bible does have some clear messages to parents on the subject. Some group debate and discussion is healthy, but don't allow one person to dominate the discussion or pressure others into ascribing to her parenting philosophy. Remember, this study is less about the hows of parenting and more about the whys.

Leading an Online Study

Those who choose to lead a study online may benefit from having an already established platform such as a blog or Facebook page. Online leaders should be prepared to post a welcome/informational post, provide a way for participants to sign up, and give encouragement to their groups during the challenge.

Participants should meet together online for approximately six weeks. Below is a sample schedule, but feel free to change it to meet the needs of your group.

Sample Schedule

Before the study starts, plan to prepare a welcome message for your participants, sharing a little of your personal story and why this study is important to you. Make sure to give them clear instructions on how to sign up for the study and a schedule of what they can expect. I suggest keeping sign-ups simple, like leaving a comment on your blog (with an email address), or having them sign up through a free online mail service (MailChimp, for example), but be sure to have them provide a way (like their email addresses) that allows you to keep up with them and contact them with other information.

Week One: Participants should read the Foreword and "Boys Are a Battle Zone" before the meeting and come prepared to discuss this material.
Homework: Read "What Is Prayer, and Why Should We Do It?"

Week Two: Discuss the contents of "What Is Prayer, and Why Should We Do It?"
Homework: Read "Going It Alone."

Week Three: Discuss the contents of "Going It Alone."
Homework: Begin the 21 Days of Prayer for Sons challenge, praying the prayers for one topic each day, ten times a day (chapters 1–7).

Week Four: Use the questions at the end of chapters 1–7 to help the participants dig into the prayer topics a little deeper (see Facilitating Online Discussions below for more information).
Homework: Pray the prayers for one topic each day, ten times a day (chapters 8–14).

Week Five: Use the questions at the end of chapters 8–14 to help the participants dig into the prayer topics a little deeper (see Facilitating Online Discussions below for more information).
Homework: Pray the prayers for one topic each day, ten times a day (chapters 15–21).

Week Six: Use the questions at the end of chapters 15–21 to help the participants dig into the prayer topics a little deeper (see

Facilitating Online Discussions below for more information). Wrap up the study.

Helpful Hints

Try to stay ahead at least one day in preparing your content so you will have plenty of time to respond to your members during the day. Try getting up in the morning thirty minutes earlier than usual to respond to emails, comments, status updates, or tweets. Do the same thing during the middle of the day and again at night. (Remember to pray for your own sons or grandsons!) This keeps you from being consumed with the challenge (and neglecting your other responsibilities) and gives you plenty of time to attend to the needs of your members.

Steps to Online Success:

1. In your welcome post, share information that will help your members get to know you better. Tell them how many sons or grandsons you have and why you are passionate about this study. Help them get excited about their participation in the challenge and provide clear ways for them to respond to each other.

2. Remind them you want them to share how this challenge is blessing and/or convicting them as parents AND as children of God.

3. If you're hosting through a blog, consider hosting a link-up each Friday so moms can write their own posts about the challenge and encourage one another by visiting each other's blogs.

4. Commit to responding to as many comments, updates, or tweets as you possibly can during the day to build a sense of community around the challenge.

5. Engage your group in as many ways as you can.

Leader's Responsibilities

The leader should be someone with at least one son or grandson (any age). She needs to be interested in exploring the place of prayer in raising godly sons and long for more dependency on God in her parenting. Leaders need not be perfect parents (as if any such thing exists) and do not have to be seasoned moms of older boys. A heart that has been prepared by God and is available, vulnerable, and teachable is more important. Leaders must be committed to seeing the prayer challenge through to its end and encouraging group members to keep going even when they're tempted to quit. Leaders should commit to praying daily for the group during the study, and also

- Provide administrative leadership (organizing and keeping momentum alive for the group).
- Meet weekly with their group.
- Promote the study and make enrollment easy.
- Make sure all participants have copies of the book.
- Provide daily encouragement via email or some type of online forum.
- Take prayer requests from the group and lift them up daily.
- Provide a sense of community (responding to comments, questions, etc.).
- Promote fellowship in any way possible among group members.
- Take notice of opportunities for ministry.

Facilitating Online Discussions

The purpose of online discussions is to begin applying what is learned during the week to everyday life. Members should be encouraged to share how God is working in their lives or their sons' lives, new things they've learned from reading the prayer Scriptures daily, and how God is changing their views of the place of prayer in parenting. While offering help to other moms is encouraged, group discussion is not intended to be a time to assert one parenting philosophy over another. *Praying for Boys* is not so much a book about the hows of parenting as it is the hows and whys of prayer. Encourage moms to take their eyes off of their own parenting skills during this time and to place them on the God who can turn hearts of stone to hearts of flesh (Ezekiel 36:26).

Decide how you will feel comfortable asking for prayer requests from your group. Do you want them to email you directly? Do you want them to post them in a comment on your Facebook page or blog? Whatever you decide is okay, but it's always best to have a plan before you get started.

Use the questions at the end of each of the main chapters to aid in your discussion when necessary.

Make members feel as comfortable as possible. Remember, you are not required to teach your members how to be good mothers; rather, your job is to encourage them to share based on their experience of the material from *Praying for Boys*. If at any time you feel unqualified to deal with a situation in your group, don't hesitate to call in the help of your pastor or other responsible authority.

If, during the course of your study, you become aware that a group member is unsaved, commit to speaking with her about it privately. Listen to the Holy Spirit and decide how you will approach her.

Define clear boundaries with your group members. This is vital to the group dynamic! Don't allow any one member to take over the group or control the comments. Gently redirect her back to the material. If more action is required, email the member privately. If a member becomes hostile or abusive in any way, gently remind her to be kind and compassionate toward the group members. If the behavior persists, ask her to leave the group.

A Note on Confidentiality

A member's ability to feel safe in sharing her heart and prayer needs is absolutely crucial to the group dynamic, but it is difficult to maintain confidentiality on a public blog (it's much easier on a private Facebook page or group). Always give your participants the option of commenting anonymously.

A Note on Parenting Styles

There are as many different parenting styles as there are models of cars, but the Bible does have some clear messages to parents on the subject. Some group debate and discussion is healthy, but don't allow one group member to dominate the discussion or pressure other members into ascribing to her parenting philosophy. Remember that this study is less about the "hows" of parenting, and more about the "whys."

Christian Standards for Social Media

Use your own judgment when it comes to handling comments, updates, or tweets that cause difficulties for your group. Consider the guidelines we're given as Christians in Matthew 18 and commit to speaking to the person alone first. DON'T use your blog, Facebook page, or Twitter account as a platform to talk about group disagreements. Here are some thoughts from my own personal experience on this subject.

Someone said something kind of ugly about me the other day and it hurt my feelings.

Actually, to be more accurate, reading it kind of sucked the breath right out of me. And I wondered why? Why would someone take the time to say something negative about me in a way that the whole world could see? I immediately went to Twitter and started typing, but I knew I couldn't publish my first response. I deleted and tried again. And deleted and tried again. And again and again and again. I did end up tweeting something about what had just happened . . . but the actual words that went out to the general public were nothing like those first ones I really wanted to tweet.

Why?

Because I had a realization—a Holy Spirit moment of restraint. Consider this: As Christians who use social media, we are held to a different standard than those who don't share our faith. Freedom of speech, brutal honesty in the name of #JustSaying, and feeling the need to share our opinions about everything just do not apply to the Christian blogger, no matter what our niche.

We are ambassadors for Christ. So perhaps it would help to take a look at how Jesus responded when He was mocked, spit upon, and hurt just for the sake of hurting.

> And the high priest stood up and said, "Have you no answer to make? What is it that these men testify against you?" But Jesus remained silent.
>
> Matthew 26:62–63

Friends, as Christians living in the social media world, the most important thing we can do is represent Christ and His Word well.

When we're feeling the desperate need to share our side of the story, let's ask ourselves why. Is it because we want to avenge ourselves? Is it because we want the other party to feel the same pain and hold them publicly accountable for their sin? Kingdom work demands something different.

Moses said to the people, "Fear not, stand firm, and see the salvation of the LORD, which he will work for you today. For the Egyptians whom you see today, you shall never see again. The LORD will fight for you, and you have only to be silent."

Exodus 14:13–14

Apply the Word of God and its instructions for life to your public persona. Shake off the feeling of freedom that social media brings. Freedom to say what you want, how you want. Freedom to hurt others and criticize them publicly instead of following the guidelines of Matthew 18. Freedom to say whatever is on your mind at the moment without first submitting it to the lens of Scripture.

Today's techno world makes it very easy to be accountable to a large number of co-laborers who share your vision and heart. But it also makes it easy to feel like you have the right and the perfect place to shout out your opinions because you have a right to your own feelings.

We don't. We've been bought. Paid for. Loved with an everlasting love and set upon a rock.

So if there is any encouragement in Christ, any comfort from love, any participation in the Spirit, any affection and sympathy, complete my joy by being of the same mind, having the same love, being in full accord and of one mind. Do nothing from selfish ambition or conceit, but in humility count others more significant than yourselves. Let each of you look not only to his own interests, but also to the interests of others. Have this mind among yourselves, which is yours in Christ Jesus, who, though he was in the form of God, did not count equality with God a thing to be grasped, but emptied himself, by taking the form of a servant, being born in the likeness of men. And being found in human form, he humbled himself by becoming obedient to the point of death, even death on a cross. Therefore God has highly exalted him and bestowed on him the name that is above every name, so that at the name of Jesus every knee should bow, in heaven and on earth and under the earth, and every tongue confess that Jesus Christ is Lord, to the glory of God the Father.

Philippians 2:1–11

The most important advice to remember, no matter how you lead your study, is to keep your eyes on Christ and help your participants do the same. Don't worry about if or how your participants respond, or the level of online community you're able to develop. Just be faithful to what God has called you to do and let Him take care of the rest. Remember, we might just change the world as we pray for our sons!

Acknowledgments

There is no way I could ever have written this book without the army of people who supported me and helped out along the way.

To my husband, the man I've had a crush on since the third grade, I am so grateful your mama taught you to work hard and just do what needs to be done without worrying about whose job it is. Your work ethic and desire to be a blessing to me and an amazing father to our two sons is nothing short of inspiring. Thank you for just letting me go write when I needed to and taking care of all the details I left behind for a short time. I love you deeply.

To my sweet boys, you are the main inspiration for this book, and I'm so grateful for the gift of the two of you. I long to see you worship at the feet of Jesus one day, and see you grow into strong, good, godly men who will impact the world with a message of truth and love. My prayer for you, sweet ones, is that you would know and follow the most amazing example of manhood we have—Jesus. I love you to the moon and back.

To my mom and dad, thank you for inspiring me to be a good mother and for keeping our boys for me once a week so I could have a writing day. There's no way I could've done this without your help.

To my grandmother Catherine Trout Lloyd, I would love so much to have an hour of your time to talk about raising good men. Although that will never happen this side of heaven, you left three good men behind, including my father, who were the evidence of your sacrifice, deep love, and hard work. Their lives tell your story. "Thank you" just doesn't cut it.

To the amazing Raising Boys Media team, especially Erin Mohring and my MOB Society writers, you are my heart! I'm so grateful for your prayers, encouragement, and belief in me and what God wanted to do with this little vision to inspire moms of boys to pray. Thank you for giving of yourselves daily so that boy-moms have a place to come to find help.

To my special group of prayer warriors—Jamie Soranno, Meggen Devlin, and Angie Yates—thank you for tolerating my crazy dreams and for believing in this message as much as I do. You are such a tremendous blessing to me.

To Kristina Tanner, thank you for your invaluable insight and feedback on the "Going It Alone" chapter. You are brave and strong, and I admire you.

To my launch team . . . Wow! Thank you for your amazing insight into the marketing of this book and for all of your contributions to make it a success. I'm grateful for each of you!

To my blogger friends—I think, more than anybody else on the planet, you guys get me. Thank you so much for believing in me and supporting me with your own platforms and wisdom. You're the best. Stacey Thacker, thank you for encouraging me to step into the role God was calling me to. I love you dearly.

To Cliff Graham, thanks for believing in "my baby" and for encouraging me to fight for it.

To the men who answered my brief survey and helped me understand the male heart, thank you!

To my agent, Chip MacGregor, thank you for taking a risk and believing in me.

To the entire Bethany House Publishing team—you should know that I prayed for over a year for you before we even "met." I told God I didn't want to publish this book if I couldn't find a house who believed in its message at least half as much as I did, and He provided you. To Jeff Braun, you reached out and took a chance. I can't tell you how much your support has meant to me. Thank you. To Andy McGuire, thanks so much for your grace-filled approach to working with authors. You've been a delight to work with on this book, and I'm grateful for you.

To my readers, I still feel like I need to pinch myself to believe that you would trust me enough to read what I write. Thank you so much for your faith, not in me, but in God's ability to work through whatever I can offer Him. I have so little to give, but He's always faithful to take our offerings—especially the ones that bring us pain—and make them into something beautiful. You are a gift to me.